Joe Stahlkuppe

Pomeranians

Everything About Purchase, Care, Nutrition, Breeding, Behavior, and Training

With illustrations by Michele Earle-Bridges
and 30 Color Photos
Consulting Editor: Matthew M. Vriends, Ph.D

BARRON'S

All inquiries should be addressed to:
Barron's Educational Series, Inc.
250 Wireless Boulevard
Hauppauge, NY 11788

International Standard Book No.
0-8120-4670-6

Library of Congress Catalog Card No. 91-14933
CIP

Library of Congress Cataloging-in-Publication Data

Stahlkuppe, Joe.
Pomeranians : everything about purchase, care, nutrition, breeding, behavior, and training / Joe Stahlkuppe ; with illustrations by Michele Earle-Bridges and color photos by well-known photographers.
p. cm.
Includes index.
ISBN 0-8120-4670-6
1. Pomeranian dogs. I. Title.
SF429.P8S73 1991   91-14933
636.7′6—dc20   CIP

Printed and Bound in China
678 4900 9

Advice and Warning:

This book is concerned with selecting, keeping, and raising Pomeranians. The publisher and the author think it is important to point out that the advice and information for Pomeranian maintenance applies to healthy, normally developed animals. Anyone who acquires an adult dog or one from an animal shelter must consider that the animal may have behavioral problems and may, for example, bite without any visible provocation. Anxiety-biters are dangerous for the owner as well as the general public.

Caution is further advised in the association of children with dogs, in meeting with other dogs, and in exercising the dog without a leash.

Photo credits:
Michele Earle-Bridges: page 10 bottom; page 27 top right, bottom; page 28, inside back cover, back cover top right, bottom right.
Gary Ellis: page 9; back cover top left.
LCA (Eugene Butenas): page 10 top, page 27 top left, back cover bottom left.
Wim van Vught: front cover; pages 45, 46, 63, 64, inside back cover.

Contents

Contents

Foreword

There seems to be some doubt among Pomeranian fans as to whether they are owners of, or are owned by, Pomeranians. I have been around purebred dogs all my life and never have I seen a breed that can boast the owner-breeder loyalty of the Pomeranian! These diminutive dogs of the north don't just win admirers or friends, they captivate those who get to know them. Royalty or commoners, the Pom doesn't seem to mind as it exerts an almost hypnotic influence over its supporters, of which I am now a helpless member.

In this book, I have attempted to provide a realistic view of the privileges and responsibilities of owning a Pomeranian. I readily admit that I don't believe this breed is for everyone. I also have tried to steer the potential Pomeranian buyer through the mazes of self-assessment, breed constraints, and economic reality.

In the show ring, the Pomeranian gives good account of itself. Competition that wears some dogs to a frazzle in the "human-eat-human" competition seems not to phase the Pom. A born showman, the Pomeranian is a breed bred for the ring. At its brushed and coiffed best, the Pomeranian is a strong competitor for the prize against any other breed at any other time.

As an obedience dog, the Pom has achieved in an arena where some other toy breeds rarely enter. Using its keen alertness and trainability, the Pomeranian radiates a confident charm as it goes through the various commands and exercises. Not hampered by its small size, the Pom is the very picture of happy persistence as it follows its beloved owner's instructions.

It is, of course, as a companion and a pet that this little dog with the big heart excels.

Although not a suitable dog for a very small child, there are very few others that could not become members of the "Pom people" throng. A good apartment roommate, the Pomeranian is quite willing to share space with any responsible tenant. In the suburbs, the Pom is able to add a yard to its domain. In a rural setting, Pomeranians can function well.

On the weekend this was written, a prestigious medical research facility released some startling information about senior citizens and their pets. Although all pets help to reduce stress, this study found that, on an annual basis, older people who had dogs visited the hospital markedly *less* than people of the same age without dogs. The videofilm accompanying the story of this study and its results shows a tall, grizzled, old gentleman bundled up in what could have been a longshoreman's outfit walking his dog—a perky, happy Pomeranian.

I would like to thank all those countless Pom people who took time to share their stories, feelings, and concerns with me. I would like to thank my wife, Cathie, and son, Shawn, for the valuable contributions they made to this book.

Much appreciation also goes to my friend, Dr. Matthew Vriends, for his undying enthusiasm and continental good humor during this project. Thanks go to a great number of veterinarians, dog groomers, and dog lovers who gave of their experience so generously.

Lastly and without apology, I would like to thank the Pomeranians themselves for living up to their accolades and for making life better in many, often subtle ways for the people who know, love, and care about them.

Joe Stahlkuppe

Understanding The Pomeranian

Origin and History of the Breed

It is ironic that such an open and clearly people-oriented little dog should have a history so shrouded by time and a lack of actual information. But such is the case of the Pomeranian, which takes its name from vague references to the old German province of Pomerania. It was from this Baltic-bordering and obscure region that early specimens of little spitz dogs were purported to originate.

Breed historians, however, are quick to point out there also exist depictions of small dogs remarkably similar to the modern Pom that have been found on vases and walls uncovered in a number of excavations of tombs dating back thousands of years in exotic locales like ancient Greece.

Unclear heritage notwithstanding, the Pomeranian owes much of its current genetic makeup to that diverse group of sledding, hunting, and herding dogs that sprang from northern Europe, commonly lumped together as the spitz. Its relatives, the Samoyed, the Norwegian elkhound, and a number of other northern breeds certainly have proven their worth as workers, companions, and pets. Even the Pomeranian's "big brother"—the keeshond (once bearing the none-too-flattering name of "the overweight Pomeranian" by early English dog breeders), fits neatly into the worker-companion-pet spitz category.

Seemingly stemming from trusted working stock, another Pomeranian irony is that the Pom, as we know it today, is largely a British re-creation complete with ties to the royal family! Queen Victoria, having been exposed to the charm of the little spitz dogs by her German grandmother Queen Charlotte, returned from Italy in 1888 with a smallish spitzlike dog that had become a favorite of hers. So captivated was Victoria that she began breeding and exhibiting specimens of what had come to be called Pomeranians. Her dogs were smaller than the sturdy, 30-pounders of the time (which more closely resembled today's German spitz and American Eskimo dogs than the modern "teacup" Poms). As a result of her interest in the breed, changes took place that would forever restructure the Pomeranian. The 30-pound (13.6 kg) spitz dog of Queen Victoria's grandmother began its transformation into the lighter Pomeranian, sometimes weighing only about one-tenth as much.

The dog-loving public in England (and later in the United States) that had taken the name of a remote German province and shortened it into the fashionable Pom nickname, proceeded to do essentially the same thing with

Pomeranians descend from the same sturdy, working stock as the keeshond and the Norwegian elkhound. Queen Victoria's interest in smaller Pomeranians did much to shape the breed into the popular companion and pet it is today.

Understanding The Pomeranian

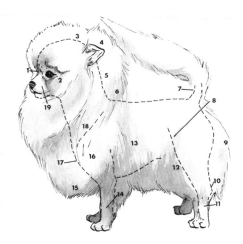

Parts of a Pomeranian.
1. stop 2. cheek 3. skull 4. ears 5. neck 6. withers 7. tail 8. loin 9. hindquarters 10. hock 11. rear pastern 12. stifle 13. ribcage 14. front pastern 15. forequarters 16. shoulder 17. chest 18. brisket 19. muzzle

the breed itself. Without losing the jaunty spitz dog confidence and charisma, English dog breeders isolated on the smallness craze and "breed 'em down in size" became the fancier's credo!

As with most fads, saner heads (and genetic practicality) finally prevailed and the Pomeranian size slide halted at about 5 pounds (2.3 kg) for a number of years. De-emphasizing diminutive size gave these early breeders the opportunity to develop other characteristics, like improved coat quality, type, and symmetry. The German spitz dog thus became the raw ore into which the skillful British dog breeders molded the Pomeranian. It was the English product that was exported to the United States in 1892 where the sprightly, little breed soon developed (and has since maintained) a strong, dedicated following.

Unlike other breeds where exaggeration of some particular facet of the breed's makeup (as is true with the decreasing Pom size) would allow unwanted temperament or hidden structural flaws to take root, the Pomeranian attracted friends not only to its tiny size and inborn sense of style, but also to its stable, companionable behavior. British dog fanciers created a beautiful miniature without sacrificing the attributes that had made the Pom's ancestors valuable workers in a much harsher environment. This near-perfect product mixture of attractiveness, alertness, and adaptability combined in this little, big dog to make the Pomeranian a winner—wherever it went!

The Nature of the Pomeranian

Whereas the Pomeranian may attract attention because of its appearance, it turns onlookers into admirers and admirers into Pom owners because of its unique personality and an almost eerie ability to relate to its human beings. The latter quality is carried over from its ancestors' long association with humans and remains not only much intact in the modern Pomeranian, but also remains close to the surface. The camaraderie with humans is one of the many reasons that Pom people tend to remain Pom people. Although Pomeranian owners readily admit that they may admire other dog breeds, they agree almost to a person, that for them the Pomeranian has something special. Most fanciers of this mighty mite back up their feelings with strong breed loyalty, and many cannot even envision their lives without a Pom in there somewhere!

Pomeranians are very bright, both in intelligence and in personality. As such, they need consistent human care and interaction to ensure that this quick-minded little dog picks up the right habits and the correct behaviors.

Understanding The Pomeranian

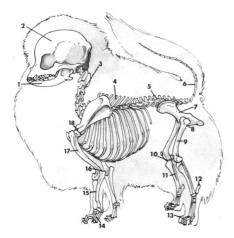

The skeletal system of a Pomeranian.
1. lower jaw (mandible) 2. skull (cranium) 2. cervical vertebrae 4. thoracic vertebrae 5. lumbar vertebrae 6. tail vertebrae 7. pelvis 8. hip joint 9. femur 10. knee joint (stifle) 11. tibia and fibula 12. hock (tarsas) 13. metatarsals 14. metacarpals 15. radius and ulna 16. elbow 17. humerus 18. shoulder joint

Usually extremely easy to housebreak, Poms have an almost catlike cleanliness. Their keen alertness makes them easy to train. In fact, many Pomeranians excel in the obedience ring, where their saucy style and happy nature garner them many fans from among the ringside audience.

Whether achieving in formal obedience work or not, the well-trained and well-socialized Pomeranian has no superior as a companion dog. Its alertness and brave, little heart make a Pom a fine early-warning watchdog quite capable of raising a bristling and outraged alarm at the first sign of an intruder. Appropriate training and encouragement will show a young Pom the difference between a legitimate cause for a barking warning and the ordinary "things that go bump in the night,"

but which pose no danger to the dog or to its household.

Many dog breeders assert that the Pomeranian has canine insight into the moods and feelings of its owner. This apparent empathy causes many Pom owners to cite instances in which their pets have picked up on subtle cues in a room or in a situation and acted in an appropriate manner. One owner, long accustomed to the same routine after work each night, found that his female Pomeranian also knew the schedule and would let out a bark if the owner strayed too far off the established time line. This behavior gives new meaning to the term watchdog!

Characteristic Pom Behavior

Pomeranians quickly put to rest any thought that they are merely animated stuffed animals totally dependent on their master or mistress in every aspect of life. Pomeranians are pert, alert, unafraid little dogs that possess clearly defined personalities that often seem to hark back to their northern dog ancestry. Poms behave much like their larger counterparts do, and often in an extremely independent fashion.

Pomeranians have a strong sense of personal property and especially enjoy their own special place or den within the home. This tendency greatly eases crate training and housebreaking. Poms also take much pride in

No breed is better able to delight and charm than the ▶ bright and perky Pomeranian puppy. These especially appealing young Poms show this canine charisma quite well.

Understanding The Pomeranian

ownership of their belongings—toys, food and water dishes, or other items possessing a value known only to the dog alone! Although they are not quarrelsome in multi-dog households, Pomeranians do seem to want to make sure that their unique role in the home and their personal items are left undisturbed.

Pom owners have noted marked fastidious eating habits on the part of their dogs. One longtime Pom fan stated that every Pomeranian he had ever owned would always take small bites of food from the food bowl, retreat a certain distance away, and enjoy the morsels at leisure. This interesting behavior may be yet another throwback to the northern dog heritage of the Pomeranian. The noted author, Jack London, describes just such behavior in some of his discussions of sled dogs, especially in the classic *The Call of the Wild.* (Of further interest is the fact that one of the key canine characters in the story was a sled dog called Spitz, a name still associated in the not-too-distant history of the Pomeranian.)

Another possible carryover from sled dog origins may be the evident love that most Poms seem to have for traveling. Especially if proper safeguards are taken, the Pomeranian makes an excellent pet for those who like to be accompanied by their dog on short trips or even on more extended vacations. The Pomeranian is small, clean, interested in its surroundings, and adaptable—all good tourist attributes!

The Pomeranian possesses a keenness of mind and a sweetness of spirit that has en-

Underneath the impressive Pomeranian coat is a short-bodied, but muscular little dog. The muscle structure of the Pom clearly reveals the miniature sled dog physique.

deared the breed to millions of people the world over. Its behavior seems consistent with its reputation as a superb companion dog. The Pomeranian is seemingly blessed with a sense of propriety and its behavior rarely is out of step with the situation. Poms are fun-loving dogs when fun is the order of the day and yet they can be more sedate when events demand calmer or quieter actions. Owners of Pomeranians who have suffered a family death or some other loss have reported clearly sympathetic behavior from their dogs when sadness has been evident. Even Pom puppies seem to show this tendency. One owner reported an extremely reserved atmosphere surrounding a litter on the day one puppy had left for a new home.

An unusual story of one Pomeranian owner illustrates the breed's kinship with human attitudes. A young Pom was owned by an elderly

◀ Though quite capable of amusing itself, Poms love company—both canine and human. Of course reasonable precautions must be taken when the Pomeranian confronts a larger dog for the first time.

person who suddenly became gravely ill. Very little hope was held out for recovery and family members were summoned to the sick person's home. Throughout the ordeal, the normally lively Pomeranian had been very staid and reserved, but at some point its behavior changed. The little dog began to bark and run excitedly about the floor near the sickbed. The dog's owner opened his eyes and smiled at the little dog—the first sign of recovery that brought the owner several more years of relatively good health and definitely good companionship from his Pom. Family members believe the little dog actually sensed the improvement in his owner and reacted to it!

The Pomeranian is brave, but rarely foolhardy. It will bristle and make its presence known to strangers or potential enemies. The Pom's actions are such that it stays just out of harm's way while actively making its displeasure abundantly clear. Normally a friendly and happy dog, the Pomeranian will make friends on its own terms and only after it is sure of one's intentions. Because of its intelligence and its high activity level, the Pomeranian needs to have its brightness and energy channeled into appropriate behaviors. With some simple, yet consistent, training, the Pom can become an excellent watchdog discerning unusual sounds from the ordinary. The genetic capacity that has made the Pomeranian a good obedience trial dog, also makes it a faithful protector of its domain.

No dog is more devoted to its owner than is the Pomeranian. The breed's adaptability allows the Pom to fit into an apartment, a suburban duplex, or a rural home. Although constraints *must* be placed on very young children (as they must with any of the toy breeds), the Pomeranian can become an excellent child's pet as well as an incomparable companion for an older person. Given the almost uncanny ability of these little dogs to pick up on certain cues and learn quickly what is expected of them, there are few breeds that can boast an overall better record of satisfied owners than can the Pomeranian. As has been mentioned, this loyalty is amply demonstrated by the number of people who, after having owned a Pom, stay with the breed—enthusiastically!

Vocal Expression

Pomeranians can be, and often are, vocal little dogs. Their basic alertness makes them prone to barking if something seems amiss. It is important that Poms be given adequate training to help them avoid becoming nuisance barkers. Whereas one Pomeranian may be a "yapper" and the next 25 bark only when it is appropriate to do so, consistent training is *always* a valuable aid. A lack of training is probably the reason for most of the Poms who have been classified as noisy (as is probably the case with noisy dogs of any breed).

Longtime breeders have numerous stories of their Poms seeming to be attempting some form of vocal communication with their owners. The earlier reference made to the Pom owner whose little female kept him on schedule may be an example of just such behavior. When this man arrived home each evening, he would go through a set of routine activities (removing his work clothes, showering, eating dinner) before he could relax and spend time with his dog. She would follow his progress through each activity. If he spent a little too much time in the shower or lingered too long over dessert, the little Pom would begin to make muttering noises that would end with a sharp yelp, reminding him to get a move on! Her owner could clearly differentiate between her monitoring behavior and a bark to alert him to some outside noise.

Understanding The Pomeranian

Pom Adaptability

One of the strongest attributes of the Pomeranian is its ability to fit into its environment. To this end, it amply uses the mental and physical capacities it is endowed with, as the sections that follow will bear out. Breeders and owners like to point out how well the Pom does in obedience work, in the show ring, as a companion dog, and as an alert home watchdog. Not surprisingly, these people are convinced about the Pom. It is therefore interesting to note how many non-Pomeranian owners have recognized the adaptability of the Pom. Veterinarians, dog groomers, dog show officials, and others who are outside Pomeranian circles are often strong in their praise of the breed, claiming almost as many superlatives for Pomeranians as do the Pom people themselves. Few people who get to know Poms have other than positive feelings about them. This speaks well for the image the little dogs have established on their trips outside their homes. Some of the staunchest supporters of the breed (other than breeders and owners, of course) are those who have seen Poms in a different light from that of their masters or mistresses. Even casual observers, who would be the most likely objective viewers of any breed, have a high positivity quotient about Pomeranians.

This adaptability of the Pomeranian was one of the reasons that British royalty was initially attracted to the little spitz dogs. That same adaptability remains one of the great strengths of the breed today and one of the key reasons for the widespread acceptance of the Pomeranian.

Pomeranian Mental Ability

Although the physical attractiveness of the Pomeranian, especially of puppies and show

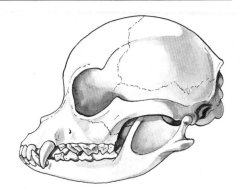

A Pomeranian's head should be wedge-shaped but not domelike, which would detract from the desired foxlike expression. The muzzle should have an abrupt stop, but not be snipy.

dogs, could account for a certain portion of the breed's great popularity, appearance is certainly not the sole reason. Cuteness and overall beauty will only go so far in assuring owner loyalty, either to an individual dog or to a specific breed.

The large number of Poms in the obedience ring speaks volumes about the way owners view the mental capacities of their little dogs. Success in this endeavor also strengthens the public perception of the Pom's intelligence and trainability. Obedience work, done in strict accordance with stringent rules and procedures, is also under the ever-watchful eye of the ringside crowd. An opportunity to shine can quickly turn into a chance to do poorly— all right out there in public! That Poms (and their owners) are willing and able to sustain themselves and even thrive in this environment gives good evidence of the smarts of the breed.

Other, less formal and less structured proof comes from Pomeranian owners and breeders. *Every* Pom owner seems to have an entire collection of stories illustrating great Pom mental

Understanding The Pomeranian

acuity. Another of the reasons cited by Queen Victoria for her attraction to and championing of the breed was its intelligence.

Stories about Pomeranians remembering long-past rewards or insults are in nearly every owner's repertoire. One Pomeranian owner related a tale of a Pomeranian who had been insulted or mistreated as a puppy by its owner's neighbor. The neighbor subsequently moved away from the area not long after the incident. Ten years later, the culprit came back for a visit. The Pom, now a graying oldster, not only remembered the long-absent neighbor, but after showing much displeasure at the visit, went to its special hiding place and could not be coaxed out until the offending person (who recalled the unintended insult of a decade before) had departed.

Pomeranians are very smart and as such bring a special responsibility to their owners (or would-be owners). In order for this little dog to become the super pet, obedience dog, show dog, or all-around companion that it can be, the Pom will need consistent treatment and adequate training.

Pom Body Language

You have but to see a Pomeranian "strut its stuff" down an aisle at a dog show or "do its thing" in an obedience trial, to know that this tiny dog has a definite physical presence that almost magnetically draws the attention of onlookers. Pom exhibitors claim that many Pomeranians rise to such occasions and actually show great enjoyment in being in the public eye.

Pomeranians, although not normally hostile to other dogs, are not passive whiners either. When encountering a larger dog, the Pom may often bristle up its stiff and considerable coat, as if to make itself appear as large

as possible. The Pomeranian will stand its ground, but this is not a stupid breed. The Pom will not normally seek a conflict if other options are available.

This behavior again seems to stem from actions commonly observed in other members of the extended spitz family of breeds. Initially, while in usually rough conditions, these Pomeranian ancestors were worker—sled dogs and indiscriminate battling was absolutely not to be tolerated. Dogs were valuable workers and fighting wasted both time and dogs. The Pom may have gained its "discretion is the better part of valor" approach from this ancestral source.

Human strangers often get much the same reception from the Pomeranian. The Pom will make its presence known, remaining a safe distance away, clearly analyzing the human being as to intent. As mentioned, the Pom remembers its friends and its foes. This memory makes early and consistent socialization and training of puppies all the more essential. A lack of awareness by someone with such a perceptive (and remembering) little dog can lead to lingering misunderstandings. Whereas some breeds will accept almost any person as an immediate friend, the Pom is a bit more reticent and cautious. This is clearly illustrated in the Pom's body language.

When confronted with a new person, the Pom often will dance away from early attempts by a stranger to pet it or to pick it up. This is seen in even very young puppies who will stay coyly just out of reach until, almost as if by some secret signal, acceptance is bestowed upon the human. The boundaries and "no man's land" imposed by the Pom become decreasingly smaller until the friendly dog or puppy is within easy grasp. The Pomeranian loves attention and petting, but by this "come hither, go yonder" routine makes it clear that any interaction will be strictly on the dog's terms!

14

Understanding The Pomeranian

Physical Aspects—The Sensory Organs

As one might suspect with any breed as keen and bright as the Pomeranian, the breed possesses exceptional sensory abilities. The terms alert and foxlike have been used aptly to describe the Pom. These terms scarcely could apply to a sluggish, inactive dog or to a member of a breed that fashion had left less-than-ready to face the world by adding sensory inhibiting flop ears or heavy bangs or other sensory undermining characteristics. Sharp eyes, excellent hearing, and a surprising acuity in sense of smell have made the Pom the aware little dog that it is.

Eyes and Ears

The eyes of the Pomeranian are among the first physical aspects that one notices about the breed. Large eyes enable the Pom to survey its domain and be instantly aware of things in its surroundings. Good eyesight is certainly one of the reasons for the Pomeranian's general excellence in the obedience ring. This intelligent little dog doesn't miss much.

The ears of the Pomeranian remain much like those of its sled dog ancestors, attractive yet utilitarian. They have not been tampered with by breeders striving to make this or that genetic fashion statement. They require no surgery or inordinate molding to make them presentable. Again, breeders are full of accounts about how Pomeranians are able to differentiate between the slightest of sounds—the step of its master on the stairs as opposed to that of a stranger or the sound of the owner's car door from the sound of all other cars. One Pomeranian had the ability to listen to the cues her mistress gave during telephone conversations to indicate when the conversation might be coming to an end. The Pom had been taught not to bark or bother her owner while the owner was on the phone. This dog became quite skillful in picking up phrases or even rises of inflection that signaled the end of the call. She would remain perfectly quiet throughout the call but, upon hearing such indicators, would let out a bark of relief often before the receiver had left the owner's ear!

In some pet breeds, natural abilities seem to have been decimated; not so with the Pomeranian. It appears to have eyesight and hearing equal to the best of its larger spitz family relatives, including those still actively used in sled dog and other work.

Senses of Smell and Taste

One breeder gives a remarkable account concerning the scenting ability of one Pom puppy. This breeder had received a pick-of-the-litter puppy in lieu of a stud fee. Only a few minutes after the puppy's arrival he was being played with by the breeder's young child on the carport of their home. Some other children from the neighborhood came by and invited the child to come with them to play ball. The child put the Pom pup back into the traveling crate in which he had arrived, and went off to play with friends. The child failed to adequately latch the crate and the pup got out. The puppy trailed his new friend nearly one-half mile! Within a few minutes, the breeder's child was astonished to see the new puppy at the ball field.

Sense of smell is another area where the Pomeranian seems to have lost none of the ancestral abilities. Scenting ability in the Pom, according to obedience people, seems to be on a par with its excellent eyesight and acute hearing.

Pomeranians have a reputation for being somewhat careful eaters. They seem to relish the taste of good, quality food while clearly rejecting more mundane fare. It would not be fair to call them picky about their food, but Poms do have definite likes and dislikes.

Understanding The Pomeranian

(Feeding will be discussed in more detail later, but this does appear to be another area where early training can get the Pom off to a good start.) A dog of any breed can be spoiled by inappropriate feeding practices that can lead to poor eating habits. With a dog as bright as the Pom, care must be taken to feed it quality food from day one and to make any dietetic changes gradually and only when necessary.

Sense of Touch

Although Poms may be somewhat reserved and guarded with strangers, once that stranger is acknowledged as a friend, the Pomeranian greatly enjoys physical contact, seeming to actually luxuriate at the touch of a favored human. This makes grooming easier with the Pomeranian than with some breeds that seem to resent the human touch (especially from a human other then their owner). Dog groomers assert that once a Pom knows and trusts a groomer, the dog often seems to relish the entire experience.

A note of caution here: The Pomeranian is a dog of heightened sensibilities. This is true of its sense of touch also. Corporal punishment may be felt by a Pom more sharply than needed or intended; especially by a young dog. It is important to note that the Pomeranian can be negatively effected by overly physical reprimanding. Small children or unthinking (or inexperienced) adults can do real damage, both physically and mentally by inappropriate swats.

When a Pomeranian Meets Other Dogs

As related earlier, the Pomeranian is a brave, but intelligent little dog. The accent here must certainly emphasize little. Whereas the Pom certainly is not foolhardy in attacking larger dogs, the Pom is still a dog and, as a dog, may decide that an attack is warranted. It is crucial that a little dog's owner recognize the danger if such a confrontation were to take place. As with small children and Pomeranians, a larger, stronger dog (perhaps not even meaning any damage) can seriously injure a 5- or 6-pound (2.3–2.7 kg) Pom. All reasonable care must be taken to lessen the chances of this occurring.

Under normal circumstances, the Pomeranian can meet and interact with other dogs without much potential jeopardy. There are always situations however, and the Pom may not always be able to skitter away from trouble. The bristling confidence of the Pom may be enough to discourage hostility in a well-behaved larger dog. Nevertheless, not every larger dog that a Pom could possibly encounter will be well behaved. With dogs of its own relative size, the Pomeranian is quite capable of maintaining its own sense of decorum. It is interesting to note that Poms in a multi-dog, multi-breed household generally serve as peacemakers rather than instigators. Several Pomeranians in a home quickly work out their own accommodations and arrangements with sled-dog-like efficiency and effectiveness.

American Kennel Club Standard for the Pomeranian

Appearance: The Pomeranian in build and appearance is a cobby, balanced, short-coupled dog. It exhibits great intelligence in its expression, and is alert in character and deportment.

Head: Well proportioned to the body, wedged-shaped but not domed in outline, with a foxlike expression. There is a pronounced stop with a rather fine but not snipy muzzle, with no lippiness. The pigment around the eyes, lips, and on the nose must be black, except self-colored in brown and blue. A round, domey skull is a major fault. Light pigment on the nose or eye rims is a major fault.

Teeth: The teeth must meet in a scissors bite, in which part of the inner surface of the upper teeth meets and engages part of the outer surface of the lower teeth. One tooth out of line does not mean an undershot or overshot mouth. An undershot mouth is a major fault.

Eyes: Bright, dark in color, and medium in size, almond-shaped and not set too wide apart nor too close together.

Ears: Small, carried erect and mounted high on the head, and placed not too far apart.

Neck and Shoulders: The neck is rather short, its base set well back on the shoulders. The Pom is not straight in shoulder, but has sufficient layback of shoulders to carry the neck proudly and high. Out at the elbows or shoulders is a major fault.

Body: The back must be short and the topline level. The body is cobby, well-ribbed, and rounded. The brisket is fairly deep and not too wide.

Legs: The forelegs are straight and parallel, of medium length in proportion to a well-balanced frame. The hocks are perpendicular to the ground, parallel to each other from hock to heel, and turning neither in nor out. The Pomeranian stands well up on its toes. Down at pasterns is a major fault. Cowhock or lack of soundness in hind legs or stifles is a major fault.

Tail: The tail is characteristic of the breed. It turns over the back and is carried flat, set high. It is profusely covered with hair.

Coat: Double-coated, a short, soft, thick undercoat, with longer, coarse, glistening outer coat consisting of guard hairs which must be harsh to the touch in order to give the proper texture for the coat to form a frill of profuse, standing-off straight hair. The front legs are well-feathered and the hind quarters are clad with long hair or feathering from the top of the rump to the hock. A soft, flat, or open coat is a major fault.

Color: Acceptable colors to be judged on an equal basis; any solid color with lighter or darker shadings of the same color, any solid color with sable or black markings, parti-color, sable and black and tan. Black and tan is black with tan or rust, sharply defined, appearing above each eye and on muzzle, throat, and forechest, on all legs and feet and below the tail. Parti-color is white with any other color distributed in even patches on the body and a white blaze on head. A white chest, foot, or leg on a whole-colored dog (except white) is a major fault.

Movement: The Pomeranian moves with a smooth, free, but not loose action. He does not elbow out in front nor move excessively wide or cowhocked behind. He is sound in action.

Size: The weight of a Pomeranian for exhibition is 3 to 7 pounds (1.4–3.2 kg). The ideal size for show specimens is from 4 to 5 pounds (1.8–2.3 kg).

Trimming and Dewclaws: Trimming for neatness is permissible around the feet and up the back of the legs to the first joint; trimming of unruly hairs on the edges of the ears and around the anus is also permitted. Dewclaws, if any, on the hind legs are generally removed. Overtrimming (beyond the location and amount described in the breed standard) should be heavily penalized.

Classifications: The Open classes at specialty shows may be divided by color as follows: Open Red, Orange, Cream and Sable; Open Black, Brown and Blue; Open Any Other Allowed Color.

Considerations Before You Buy

Is the Pomeranian the Right Dog for You?

Honesty is the key in considering your purchase of a Pom. You must set aside all those mental pictures that you may have gathered of cute Pom puppies, of a devoted Pom sharing your chair before a toasty fire in the hearth, or of the stylish pair you and your Pom will make when you go out for a walk. All of these images are certainly possible, but it is crucial for your own good and for the good of the as-yet-not bought dog that you face the realities of Pomeranian ownership.

Any dog is a living, breathing creature with needs and wants (somewhat like yourself). Before purchase of such a creature, you (and each member of your household) need to be certain that you want to assume the full-time responsibility for another dependent being for the next 10 or 12 years. Your Pom will look to you for everything—food, shelter, and care. Are you and your family willing and able to commit to this task?

The following questions (and others of your own devising) should be asked and answered before going further into Pom ownership:

- Does each person in your home know and understand what having a Pom will mean and entail?
- Does each person in your home willingly accept this job?
- Is each person willing to share time and attention with the Pom?
- Do we have the time and resources to add a Pom to our family? (At least one hour every day for care, playing, training, etc., and approximately $30 per month for quality food, veterinary care, outside grooming, etc.)?
- Do we realize that the Pom can be injured by other dogs, small children, or through thoughtless actions and are we willing to protect this canine member of our family?

This list of questions may seem obvious or even unnecessary, but failure to deal with the issues raised here can embark you and an innocent dog on a long trail of discomfort, pain, and hardship. The Pomeranian is a great companion dog and it is important that you and your family are also willing to be great dog companions.

If, after careful thought and consideration, the answer to "Is the Pomeranian the right dog for you?" is yes, then you are to be congratulated as a potential Pom owner. If the answer is no, perhaps even more congratulations are in order, for you have weighed the questions (and more importantly *your* answers) and have decided that now may not be the time for bringing a Pomeranian into your life and that of your family. In both circumstances, the goals are the same—happy ownership of a wonderful, little dog who arrives when conditions are right for it and the owner(s).

A Puppy or an Older Dog?

Part of the answer to the age of the Pom you obtain is hinged on what end purpose you have in mind for the dog. Obedience work or a dog show career can usually best be accomplished by purchasing a pup from appropriate show or obedience stock and working with that pup as it grows up. As companions, there may very well be adult Pomeranians available. (You can check with Pom breeders in your area or with the breed club.)

Bringing a puppy into your home is much like bringing a human baby into your home. This is a totally dependent entity that will need much care, love, and supervision. Like a human baby, a Pom baby will make messes, cry in the middle of the night, and require a lot of attention. A Pom baby will need to be handled gently and given the first, rudimentary

Considerations Before You Buy

When lifting a Pomeranian puppy, always place a supporting hand under the hindquarters. Remember to be gentle when handling the tiny youngster.

steps in becoming a well-trained adult Pom.

Someone, specifically, should be responsible for helping the Pom puppy adjust to its new home. This will require time and effort on this someone's part. Be certain that this someone wants to do this crucial job and is able to successfully do it.

A puppy will need consistent care, without fail, as a high priority. Perhaps the cavalryman in the Old West, who could not eat or rest until he had taken care of his horse, sets a good example for model dog owners. A puppy or an older dog should receive attention before any other activity. You brought it here, it didn't come uninvited.

An older Pomeranian may not need as much immediate attention or supervision as a puppy, but even a well-trained adult dog will need some adjustment time in its new home.

An older dog may even have a particular set of problem dynamics. It may have been mistreated and thereby be snappish and defensive. It may have been closely attached to someone in its previous home and may grieve (sometimes even to the point of risking ill health). The adult dog may have learned another schedule and have some difficulty adjusting to yours. There are any number of difficulties that can and do arise, but most of the time a skillful new owner can find a way to resolve most of them. Remember that Pomeranians are famous for their adaptability!

If you are a new dog owner or a new Pom person, perhaps the best route to take would be to start with a puppy. Books, Pom breeders, veterinarians, and other dog professionals can help you avoid major pitfalls, but only if you will listen and apply what you have learned.

Male or Female?

Both male and female Pomeranians make wonderful pets and can have sparkling careers in the obedience or show ring. Females are affectionate, feminine, and often become very attached to their families (as do males). Unless you have serious thoughts about breeding Pomeranians (which will be discussed later) then either a male or a female should do just as well.

If you choose a female and showing is not your goal, have her spayed. All the problems that can stem from your female coming "in season" will be eliminated. Spaying will keep her from being eligible for entry in a dog show. Males can also be neutered which should not affect their pet qualities and will make them more tractable if they should come into contact with unspayed females. Spayed females and neutered males can still compete in obedience trial activities. Unless you have *serious*

19

plans to enter Pom breeding, spaying or neutering your dog is a wise move.

The male Pom is all male in spite of his small size. He will have a tendency to marking his territory on walks and outings. A male can show some aggressive behavior when confronted with strange dogs, but good training and good supervision on your part can prevent any potentially dangerous confrontations with larger dogs. It is well to remember that the male Pomeranian may not always remember he is much smaller than some adversaries. As with small children, larger dogs can do severe damage to a Pomeranian. Even a playful puppy of a larger breed could hurt your Pomeranian. Guard against this by being alert to any situation where such a tragedy could occur. (Note: When bringing a Pom into a home where a cat lives, the same sort of preventive care must be undertaken. Some cats are much larger than any Pomeranian. With their prominent eyes and inquisitive nature, a Pom, especially a youngster, could sustain an eye injury from a well-aimed paw by an angry feline.)

If breeding Pomeranians seems to be an area of interest to you (but only after much careful study and consideration), you might well be advised to purchase the best quality female puppy available. If she happens to do well in the show ring or comes from an exceptional line of dogs that have done well there, you may be able to breed her to a stud dog of good repute and compatible pedigree. It is wise to remember that dog breeding is best accomplished only by serious dog breeders who have the improvement of the breed as their ultimate goal. Just breeding your Pom bitch to have her experience having puppies is an irresponsible attitude for you to take and a wise one to avoid.

Purchasing a male puppy in hopes that he will become a top producing stud dog is a true longshot. Even for lifetime Pomeranian breeders to obtain such a male puppy is rare indeed. Owning a male of lesser quality just on the off chance that someone would want to breed to him is another irresponsible attitude. To breed specifically for pet quality, when even the very best show matings produce more pet specimens than show dogs, is generally a bad idea as long as there are thousands of unwanted puppies born each year that could use loving homes.

Both male and female Pomeranians make excellent pets. The little females possess a sweetness that makes them superior pets for older people. The little males are perky chaps who have won people over who never thought they could admire, much less own, a small dog. The choice of a male or female for you, if you want a good pet, is an easy one. Just pick out the male or female that you like the best! You won't go wrong, either way.

Pet Quality or Show Quality?

It is important to decide whether you want a pet quality puppy or a show quality puppy. "Pet quality" should never be a catchall phrase for reject puppies any more than "show quality" automatically guarantees you a top show dog in the future.

Pet quality puppies may be excellent obedience dogs and can excel as personal pets. As a rule, these pups have some little conformation flaws that makes it impossible for them to be considered for the show ring. These flaws are generally cosmetic in form, like being a little too large, and should not include any physical disabilities or conditions which would make or cause such a puppy to be unhealthy or unsound. As a rule, pet quality puppies are also not viewed as potential breeding stock.

Show quality puppies are much harder to locate. Some breeders are reluctant to sell a puppy with show potential to a first time Pom owner or to an owner who may not be able to allow the puppy to reach its full showroom potential. Show quality puppies will be considerably more expensive than are pet quality puppies, but if showing your Pom is your ultimate goal, study hard and buy the best possible puppy from the best possible stock available. Occasionally breeders will make arrangements that will allow a serious dog exhibitor to own a dog in partnership with the breeder. Other similar deals also may exist if you want a breeding dog of sound show stock. These arrangements, while not common, do happen. They usually hinge on whether you possess the skill and motivation to give a show dog the best possible exposure and on whether you can convince a serious Pom breeder that you do.

Pet quality puppies, though less expensive and generally more available than show quality puppies, should be healthy, happy Poms quite capable of becoming a key part of your life. If showing (or breeding) is not in your game plan, the pet quality puppy is obviously tailored to your needs.

How To Select a Pom Puppy

Before you begin the selection process there are a number of things that will make your task easier and less of a gamble. Read as much as you can about the Pomeranian. Contact the breed clubs and breeders in your area. Visit dog shows and chat with breeder-exhibitors there. Look at their show Poms. See what the breed is supposed to look like at its very best. In short, get to know the Pom before you set out on your quest. Visually inspect as many Poms as possible and, if you have a color preference, take time to look at many dogs of the same color (a color preference is probably natural, but if you are looking for a pet and a

good one of a different color turns up, don't ignore it).

If you are after a show quality puppy, stick with quality breeders who may help you find the puppy you are seeking. Forget about bargain basement Poms that may come your way. Center your thinking not only on one specific Pomeranian, but on a specific family or "line." Concentrate your thoughts on the specific attributes you want such a puppy to possess. Find out which breeder has a top reputation (not just a top show record). Do a lot of questioning and listening and refrain from buying any puppy unless it fits the general model you have thoughtfully constructed. Even with the best breeder selling you the puppy of highest possible potential, not every such situation produces a winning show dog (and winning is the main reason dogs are shown).

To pick a show quality puppy, you would do well to make friends with a Pom breeder who can help you best apply the written descriptions in the Pomeranian Breed Standard to a young puppy. Finding the show puppy you are seeking may be a long, arduous process, but if showing is a sincere goal, it is the only way you can go about it. While most breeders are honest, helpful people, "buyer beware" is always a good motto when you are new in any interest area, including show dogs!

Finding a pet quality puppy may be much simpler, but can be as potentially risky. Just because you are planning to invest hundreds for a pet rather than thousands for a show pup doesn't mean that you should not read, study, compare, check around, and try to find the best quality puppy. (Remember that we are talking about adding a family "member" who will be with you for perhaps a decade or more. Care is the watchword!)

Pet quality Poms are available from several sources. Sometimes you can find just the pet you are seeking in a pet store. Many quality

Considerations Before You Buy

pet stores purchase pups from good breeders and will guarantee these puppies. Unfortunately, other stores obtain their stock from mass production operations in which unsound parents produce unsound offspring with little thought to the pain and heartache they could cause you over the years. Avoid them like rabies! Find a store that buys from local breeders or from kennels with good reputations. You have a much better chance with the stores that follow this approach. Insist that your pup come from a sound environment and demand proof of it. Good stores are only too happy to show that your puppy has a sound background.

A pet quality Pomeranian could come from a breeder of show stock. As many more pet puppies are produced than show pups you should be able to find a good pup from this source. In this case, you have a chance to look at your pup's environment. Ask to see the parents of the puppy. Most breeders welcome potential puppy buyers who will take the time to check things out. They know these buyers are the ones most likely to give a puppy the care it deserves. Professional dog breeders are concerned about their reputations and are also faced with finding good homes for their excess pet quality pups. While you are looking for a place from which to obtain a good pet Pom puppy, they are looking for a good owner for one of their not-quite-show specimens. This can, and often does work out for all three of you—the breeder, you, and the puppy.

Another source for a pet quality Pom is the small "backyard" breeder. This is more of a gamble than the professional breeder, but can work out well. The small breeder is that person who has a good Pomeranian female, probably as the family pet who has been bred to a good quality stud (also possibly "in the family"). You are pretty much on your own in this situation, but you do have some advantages with small breeders. They generally really care

about their Poms and the resultant puppies. Money may not be their prime motivation and you can sometimes get a good pet for less than you could under other circumstances. However, the "buyer beware" warning is also important here. If the premises are not clean or if there are more than a couple of adult dogs and the puppies, you may have stumbled into a puppy mill in the making. If the small breeder seems conscientious and the parent stock appears sound and well-adjusted, you may have a reasonable chance of getting an acceptable pet quality puppy. If the backyard breeder has taken the effort to find a really good stud dog (generally a Champion) and is keeping a puppy from the litter for him- or herself, then you are ahead of the game. Again, your knowledge of what you are seeking in a Pom will always be your best defense.

You will probably need a good pet store to serve as a source for many of the things your Pom puppy will need. Premium food, a large assortment of toys, crates, collars and leads, helpful books, and information can all be obtained at such a store. Sometimes, as mentioned, you may find Pomeranian pet quality puppies available at the pet store also.

Let the "buyer beware!" motto guide your steps in any case. If you know and trust the pet store owners and have faith in them (and a written guarantee comes with the puppy) perhaps you should add this store as a possible source for your new family member. Whatever you do, don't let a slick store layout and a persuasive salesperson on commission talk you into anything.

Many stores can help put you in touch with show dog or backyard breeders who may have the puppy you are seeking. In any case, having the friendship of a good, local pet store for supplies, information, and general advice will be very helpful.

"Diamonds in the rough" are tough (if not impossible) to find. Seek a potential show quality pup from a show-oriented breeder. An obedience trial puppy probably should come from stock that has distinguished itself in the obedience ring. Decide what you want in a puppy and then go to the place you are most likely to find it.

Whatever source you choose, take time to observe the puppies. Don't ruin all the effort you have made up to this point by fixating on one puppy and making your ideal fit that pup because it's there and so are you. Stick with your game plan and make every effort to determine if the puppies shown fit what you are seeking. Remember you are seeking a sound, healthy puppy that will be a family member/companion for years to come. If you choose impulsively now you may have a lot of time to regret it in the future.

Prior to actually choosing a puppy from any source, make sure you have three things:

1. The puppy's health records (showing dates of vaccination, deworming, and a health certificate, signed by a veterinarian stating that the puppy has been examined and appears healthy).

2. The AKC (American Kennel Club) Registration certificate stating that your Pom is a purebred. With this certificate you should also receive application papers to send to the AKC to register the puppy in your name.

3. A pedigree (which is really only as good as the source from which the puppy comes) showing the pup's parents and recent lineage. These documents are very important and if they are not available, don't buy the puppy!

Assuming that all the papers are in order and you feel that the source you have chosen will be reliable and will guarantee the puppy to be healthy and sound (always best to have in writing), the time for selection is at hand. You already have an idea of what you want (male or female, color, quality, etc.), and, one hopes you have chosen a source that will give you several puppies from which to choose.

Pomeranians usually have very small litters (one, two, or maybe three puppies), so you may have to wait to get a puppy that fits color or other specific requirements that you and your family may have. Waiting for the exactly right puppy (after you have taken the time to really decide what kind of puppy that is) should be no real problem.

Carefully handle each puppy that fits your requirements, remembering that a 6 to 8-week-old puppy will not clearly reflect all that it may become. Depending on the amount of contact with outsiders the puppies have had, the puppies may be somewhat apprehensive at your approach, but you can tell if they seem healthy and you can see if they appear sound and not overly frightened by your visit.

You may not find exactly what you are seeking, but don't be afraid to walk away. There are other puppies and this is a long term relationship you are planning. If that special puppy is there, the one that is bold, bright-eyed, and fits your requirements, you may have found your new family member. The accent is on the word may. You want to refrain from mentally and emotionally fully deciding on the puppy until *your* veterinarian has had a chance to inspect it and pronounce it sound and healthy.

Time taken now will be well worth it later, when this friendly puppy becomes the ideal companion that has been the object of all your reading, questioning, and searching.

How To Pick Up a Puppy

If you are visiting several sources looking for a Pom puppy, always wash your hands between stops. It would be sad to think that you were responsible for transmitting some disease to several litters of Pomeranian puppies.

The best way to handle a tiny Pom puppy is to gently pick it up supporting the back and

Considerations Before You Buy

Small children should always be supervised when they are playing with a Pomeranian. Fragile puppies or even older dogs can be injured by rough play.

rear end with one hand and the chest with the other. The puppy will feel supported and more comfortable.

The Pomeranian and the Small Child

Pomeranians and very small children do not mix! This is not the dog's fault, but merely a realistic assertion that small children can seriously (sometimes even fatally) injure very small dogs. Little legs can easily break with rough treatment and a little dog jumping from a child's arms can be all that it would take for the Pom to be hurt. Small children must *always* be supervised when they are playing with a Pomeranian.

Not even all older children are mature enough to be left unsupervised with a fragile Pomeranian puppy (or an adult for that matter). Let common sense guide you in these matters. The safety of your pet should be your prime concern.

The Cost of Keeping a Pom

Beyond the actual cost of purchasing a Pomeranian (an estimated $200 for a pet and up to $1,000 or more for a show prospect), a new Pom owner would be prudent to budget about $30 per month for the upkeep of the dog.

This amount would include the cost of premium dog food, regular veterinary checkups, incidental equipment, and a trip to the groomer when needed. Some dogs in some sections of the country will need a little more in this budget, some in other areas will need a little less. This will give you a starting point and some idea about the financial commitment required.

Christmas Puppies

This advice may fly in the face of tradition, your personal wishes and several other accepted ideas, but surprising someone with a puppy on Christmas morning is not a good idea. Bringing a new puppy into your home at a time when a lot of unusual activities are planned cannot help an already bewildered puppy adjust to a new environment. Give the puppy several weeks before Christmas or several weeks after Christmas when it can be the center of attention, can get the care it needs and deserves, and can realize that these new people in its life really do love it.

Caring For Your Pomeranian

Before You Bring Your Pom Home

A change of environment can be stressful for any dog. For your Pomeranian to have the best possible start in its new home, there are a number of things you can do to make the transition less traumatic.

Purchase a sturdy, flat-bottomed water bowl and a similar one for food. These should not easily turn over and yet be shallow enough for your Pom to be able to get at their contents without having to get in with the contents.

You need to obtain some of the *same* food that the puppy has been eating (change brands some other time, if you wish, but definitely not during such a trying time for your new dog).

A dog cage, crate, or carrier (see the chapter on Training Your Pomeranian) perhaps of the airline-approved type will be very helpful in fulfilling the "den" requirements so important to Pomeranians. This cage, crate, or carrier will be your dog's special place within your home. It will also be a great aid in housebreaking, as we shall soon see. Your pup will need a collar and lead of appropriate size (or perhaps a one-piece nylon collar and lead) to introduce it to the big, new world. You should also purchase a good quality grooming comb and brush. Ask the breeder or pet store to recommend a good brand.

A very important area where the breeder or pet store may be able to assist is with toys. If your Pom puppy has, while still at the breeder's or at the pet store, taken an interest in a particular toy, by all means obtain that particular toy. Pomeranians are great little possessors and such a toy would greatly help the pup (as it would an older dog) to adjust to its new home with you. If no such special interest in a particular toy has been observed, ask about the kind of toys to get.

If you have chosen a puppy and are yet to take it home, you might introduce such a plaything to your chosen puppy before it is ready to go home so that it will already be familiar. Handle the toy and have your family members handle the toy so that your scents will not be completely alien to the puppy when the time to go home with you arrives. In any case toys are essential for Poms!

Another essential is the "puppy-proofing" that must be done before you bring your Pomeranian home. This can be an interesting and enlightening experience for you. In much the same way that you might prepare a room for an active toddler, you need to go over *all* the areas in your home to which the puppy will have access for anything that could do it harm. One dog expert suggests that you actually get down on the floor and check out each room from the puppy's perspective.

You are looking for pins, needles, tacks, beads, toxic houseplants, or anything that a small, inquisitive puppy might discover and possibly chew or swallow. Also be on the lookout for exposed electrical wires or things which, if pulled on by a puppy, might fall on it. Check for exposed woodwork that, especially in older homes, may have lead-based paint or which may have been treated with some chemical polish or spray that might do harm to a young, teething puppy. Stairwells and narrow spaces behind appliances or furniture where a puppy might fall or get trapped are obvious danger areas.

Pomeranian puppies don't need to be doing much jumping. Their little legs can so easily break on what might not appear to be any distance at all (like from the sofa to the floor!). Damage can also be done to little shoulders and hips. Keep your Pom off the furniture for its sake and the furniture's!

Your Pomeranian puppy will have had limited experience outside of that gained through its mother, littermates, and the breeder. You will now have to ensure that this special puppy gets the learning opportunities it needs to avoid injury through an oversight on your part or puppyish ignorance on its part.

You have crawled all over the floor seeking potentially dangerous objects. You have closed off stairwells and other unsafe places. You have purchased the things your new puppy will need. You have reminded all members of the family that having a new puppy, literally underfoot, means new responsibilities. You have gone over a list of possible problems and assigned duties. You and the breeder or pet store have worked out a time that will be the very best for the puppy to go home with you.

You have arranged to be home for the next several days (or to have someone at home) to help the puppy adjust. You are now, by your own assessment, ready to bring your Pom puppy home!

Bringing Your Pom Puppy Home

An important way to help your new Pomeranian adjust to its new home is by purchasing a dog cage, crate, or carrier, as mentioned earlier. As with toys, you might also introduce your new puppy to this new cage, crate, or carrier even before you bring the puppy home. By taking this preliminary step, the puppy (or even an older dog) can have its own makeshift den with its own familiar scents and comforting sameness before it ever arrives at your home.

The importance of such a den to your Pomeranian cannot be overestimated. It will be your pup's own special place, a sanctuary, within your home. Such a place of warmth and safety will be crucial to your puppy's well-being. Some humans may tend to see this as locking in the dog, but the dog sees it as a way to lock the people out! In the trying times of adjusting to its new home, this den is a safe

A cage or crate becomes a Pom's own special place in your home. By taking advantage of this denning instinct, housebreaking and training are much more easily accomplished.

haven in a world that the dog may find confusing or even frightening.

For an 8-week-old puppy, the actual trip to its new home can be traumatic in itself. If possible, have a member of the family gently hold the puppy (being sure to support the pup's body from beneath while not squeezing it too tightly) during the ride (an old robe and some paper towels might not be a bad idea in the event of car sickness). If this family member could already be an "old friend" from previous visits to the pup, so much the better. Poms do love to travel, but even a short car ride to a young pup may be overwhelming. Don't get things off to a bad start.

Above: Daily brushing can be a pleasurable experience ▶ for both the owner and the Pom. Below: While the Pom is very young, start paying close attention to its feet and nails. Get your groomer or veterinarian to show you how to trim the toenails without cutting too closely.

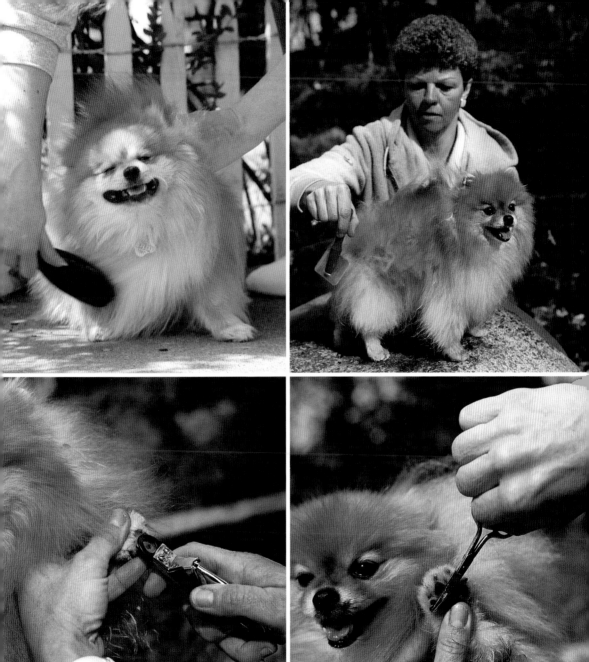

Caring For Your Pomeranian

If the journey is several hours or more, frequent stopping for "nature breaks" and to reassure the puppy are a good idea. If the puppy cannot be in someone's arms, it should be in its carrier. Don't allow the puppy to stand up or to attempt to run around in the automobile. Unexpected stops, sharp turns, or even falling off the car seat can cause injury.

When you arrive home, give your Pomeranian a chance to nose around in the outside area where you will normally be walking the pup and where you will want it to defecate and urinate. Training begins *now* by not confusing the animal about where you expect it to eliminate waste. If the puppy relieves itself in the appropriate area, praise the puppy liberally. Pomeranians are smart and it shouldn't take too long for it to associate going outside to this specific location with urination and defecation. This type of patience and consistency on your part will make housebreaking much less of a trauma for both the puppy and you!

Assuming you have pup-proofed the areas inside your home where the puppy will be allowed to enter, give your new family member some time to explore. Remember that it is still a puppy and may tire quickly. Certainly play with the puppy, but when it shows signs of tiring return it to its den. The puppy will soon learn where it is to sleep and may even soon begin to go directly there when it is tired or seeks the comfort of its own place.

◄ Above left: The most basic command, the "sit" is taught with the dog positioned near the trainer's left foot. Above right: The "down" is just an extension of the "sit." Below left: Praise from its owner is the reward most Poms cherish, but treats are also effective. Below right: The small size of the Pomeranian does nothing to diminish the flair and flash with which it goes through life.

Your puppy will now have to learn to adjust to being alone without its mother or littermates, but *you* will also have to make an adjustment. You are training your Pomeranian by your actions, and rapid learning is taking place in your young dog's fertile mind. If you are intent on crate-training (using the crate, cage, or carrier to serve as its home-within-the-home) your puppy, then you must let it know that it will not be allowed out, cuddled, petted, or fawned over when it whines or cries. You can quietly speak to the puppy to reassure it that you are there but if you do take the puppy into your arms at each cry, it will soon learn how to get into your arms—by crying!

Consistency is vital here. If you are determined (as you should be) not to give in to the wails and whimpers and some other family member slips in and takes the puppy out of its sleeping place, then all of your resolve is for nothing. No one prefers to listen to a sad, lonely puppy crying, but that puppy can become a sad, lonely adult dog still crying if consistent training is not firmly followed. Steel yourself and your family to a few nights of crying with the knowledge that, like with inoculations for disease, a little discomfort now will mean a much happier and better adjusted pet later.

There are, of course, things that can be done to make it a little easier on the puppy *within* the crate. An old-fashioned hot water bottle (nonleaking) or some toy or piece of familiar bedding can make things better. An old wind-up alarm clock, whose ticking may serve to replace the mother's heartbeat can also be an aid (make sure the alarm portion of this clock is inoperable). Some have suggested that turning on a radio on low volume to an all-night talk station can be of comfort to the puppy in falling asleep.

Feeding your new puppy should not be too difficult, but again, consistency is important. You have already obtained the same food that the puppy has been eating. Using the same food (provided the pet store or the breeder was not experiencing some food-related problem with this puppy), on the same schedule to which the puppy is accustomed, will aid in avoiding some of the transitional stress. Even with the same diet, transplanting a puppy will have some negative impact on it. Expect some minor diarrhea for a day or so (see your veterinarian if it continues more than a couple of days, especially when feeding the same diet). Keep on schedule with your pup's feedings. As with a human infant, much of the puppy's first days will be taken up with eating and sleeping. If your puppy is to adapt to its new environment quickly and easily, it will need consistency. You are the source for that.

Traveling with Your Pomeranian

Traveling with a Pom is a good deal easier than with some breeds. The Pomeranian is a highly adaptable little dog that enjoys traveling and seems to suffer few bad side effects from it. Where some dogs are stressed by a change of scenery, the Pom takes it in stride and seems to thrive on it.

There are those Pomeranian breeders who believe that the Pomeranian's good record as a show dog and as an obedience trial dog comes, at least in part, from its ability to do well in varied environments—its adaptability. Whether the Pom does well in competition on the road because it likes to travel is open to discussion. One thing is for sure; the Pomeranian can make a very good traveling buddy.

Traveling with any pet, even a good traveler like the Pom, calls for some good planning and preparations on your part. Since many Poms are crate-trained and can take their den with them, including your dog on your vacation could be a great idea!

Traveling by Air

Traveling by air with a pet has certainly changed over the years. Today, your Pom and its airline-approved carrier are welcomed on most if not all of the larger domestic and overseas airlines. (If your dog's den is something other than an approved carrier, these are available, for a fee, from the airlines.) Even though conditions are better for the flying pet now there are still some good rules to follow before your Pom takes off:

1. Well before you make reservations for yourself, check with the airlines as to their rules and suggestions about taking your pet along. Some may even let your pet ride in the passenger section with you as carry-on luggage.

2. Check with your pet's veterinarian to see if there are any reasons your Pom shouldn't make the trip. (Very young pups or older dogs might be best left at home.) The veterinarian can also provide a health certificate for your dog if the airline requires it (which they usually do and which usually must be dated no more than 10 days from the date of your trip). Ask the veterinarian about the need for tranquilizers or anti-airsickness pills for your pet.

3. Make your reservations and those for your pet well in advance of the trip date. If your pet cannot be in the passenger area with you, try to get a direct flight to your destination (even if you have to drive to the nearest hub airport to do so). This will allow you to see your pet loaded on the same plane that you board and lessen the chance of you and your Pomeranian ending up in different planes (or different cities).

4. If you are traveling to another country, be sure to meet all the entry requirements for bringing in a pet.

5. If using your own airline-approved carrier, carefully check over the carrier to see that none of the screws holding it together have loosened, that the door and latch work effectively and that it has the necessary airline "conversion kit" for a water dish that can be filled from outside the carrier.

6. Make sure that you have the "Live Animal" stickers prominently displayed on your crate along with a luggage tag with your name, your home number and a number where you can be reached in your destination city.

7. Be sure to enclose in the carrier a freshly laundered pad or blanket to make the carrier more comfortable. A favorite toy would be a nice addition.

8. Do not feed your pet for eight to ten hours prior to departure. You can, however, give it water and exercise up to two hours before boarding. Other than the external water dish, don't put food or water in the carrier. It will only be a potential mess. (You do want to be sure you have packed in your luggage enough of your Pom's regular food and any medications it may need during the trip.)

9. Have your firm but polite demeanor ready to make sure that airline personnel realize how important your Pomeranian is to you and to what lengths you will go to ensure its safety and comfort. (One frequent flyer dog breeder makes a point of taking a picture of the dog in its crate as it is being readied for loading on the flight. She claims that the existence of such photographic proof has helped her avoid many problems.)

Traveling by Car

You will make many short trips with your Pomeranian in a private automobile. While the requirements for taking your dog with you on a longer trip in your car are not as stringent as those of an airline, you would do well not to take these extended car travel precautions too lightly.

1. Always have your Pomeranian in a carrier or in a doggy safety harness when you are riding together.

2. Check with the veterinarian for some motion sickness medications. (Don't feed it 8 to 12 hours before you plan to leave and provide it water only up to 2 hours before leaving.)

3. Stop every hour or so to give the dog a breather, a drink of water and some exercise. Always use your lead when you take the dog out of the carrier.

4. *Never* leave your dog in a parked car, even with windows rolled down, during the day when the temperature is as high as 60° F (16° C) (see heatstroke).

5. If you are traveling across the country check with auto clubs and travel guides about which motels and hotels will allow pets in their rooms. You might also confirm that they allow well-behaved pets when you make reservations by phone. A little planning will make the trip safer and saner.

Never leave a dog in a parked car, *even with the windows down* on a day when the temperature is as high as 60° F (16° C). Only a very few minutes in a parked car on a warm day can kill your pet.

Caring For Your Pomeranian

Boarding Your Pomeranian

If you can't take your pet with you on your trip, then boarding it will be your alternative. This in not as bleak a prospect as you (and your Pom) might think. There are several good possibilities.

1. In many locales, pet sitters are available to take care of your pet in your own home while you are away. Usually these are skillful, caring people who can furnish numerous valid references.

2. You and your Pom may have a friend, neighbor or family member who can care for your pet. Your dog might be able to stay at home under this arrangement. This person needs to be someone the Pomeranian likes.

3. Your veterinarian or your groomer may board dogs and would be already known and accepted by your dog in a place it knows.

4. The breeder where you bought your Pom (if close at hand) may be willing to take an alumnus in as a boarder. You would be sure of good care in this circumstance.

5. There are some excellent boarding kennels that are accredited with the American Boarding Kennel Association (ABKA) (see Useful Addresses and Literature).

Feeding Your Pomeranian

The Importance of a Balanced Diet

You have gone to considerable effort to learn about and obtain a good quality Pomeranian. What you feed your Pom will be a major factor in its health (mental and physical) and in its longevity. The importance of a balanced diet and your understanding of what makes it balanced will be a key to this important part of dog ownership.

There are two rules to follow in feeding a Pomeranian: 1. Find a high quality dog food and feed it consistently; 2. Don't overfeed. (This means *no tablescraps.*)

The computer phrase "garbage in; garbage out" is also an apt point to remember about canine nutrition. Your Pomeranian will need a balanced diet to grow strong and healthy, and to develop the potential that is its genetic birthright. A poor diet can cause your Pom a legion of medical, behavioral, and developmental problems.

Avoiding a poor diet and establishing a solid nutritional plan isn't difficult. Provide your Pomeranian with a high-quality dog food and don't overfeed!

Basic Nutrition

There are seven components to a balanced diet for your Pomeranian: proteins, carbohydrates, fats, vitamins, minerals, water, and consistency/knowledge.

Protein

Protein provides the dog with amino acids that are essential for growth, the maintenance of healthy muscle and bone, the repair of that same muscle and bone, the production of infection-fighting antibodies, and production of hormones and enzymes that aid in the dog's body's chemical processes. Good sources of protein are meat and poultry products, milk products, fish meal, soybeans, and corn.

Carbohydrates

Carbohydrates provide energy to power the Pom's internal motor. Thoroughly cooked grains, starches, and vegetables provide most of the carbohydrates seen in quality dog foods. Carbohydrates are measured in calories.

Fats

Fat is another much more concentrated source of energy for your Pomeranian, which can provide more than twice as much energy as a like amount of protein or carbohydrates. Fat also provides the "delivery system" for the fat soluble vitamins, A, D, E, and K, into your Pom's system for healthy skin and coat. In addition, fat aids in maintaining a healthy nervous system and makes dog food taste better.

Vitamins

Vitamins are needed for general body functions and generally needed in small quantities which are easily provided in a balanced diet of a high-quality dog food so that additional supplementation is *not* usually needed. The best source of vitamins is from a well-balanced diet.

Feeding Your Pomeranian

Minerals

Minerals are essential for normal body functioning: Calcium and phosphorus are needed for strong bones, muscles, and teeth; potassium and sodium aid with the maintenance of a healthy nervous system and with the maintenance of normal bodily fluids; iron promotes healthy blood in your pet by transporting oxygen throughout its body.

(*Important note*: A high-quality dog food will contain the appropriate levels of both vitamins and minerals. Don't try to supplement a high-quality dog food without first consulting with your veterinarian. Both vitamins and minerals can be easily overdone.)

Water

Often the most neglected part of a dog's diet and yet a very important one is water. Your Pom will need plenty of clean, fresh water all the time. It might not hurt (you or your dog) if you had your water tested annually even if you are part of a municipal water system. With water purity a question in many communities, your actions here may be a good preventative against chemical imbalances or interactions.

Consistency/Knowledge

Another often-ignored aspect of a balanced diet is the manner in which you provide food to your dog. As with so many other areas of Pom care, consistency is important in diet as well. Find a good high-quality dog food that your pet likes and stay with it. Even experienced dog people (who should know better!) frequently pick up first this food and then that food without regard to the dog's needs. Changing from one food source to another should usually take two weeks or longer with the gradual mixing of the new food with the old in ever increasing amounts until the old is gone.

Your knowledge about canine nutrition and about dog foods can be a big help to your Pomeranian who has to depend on you.

Commercial Dog Food

There are a number of excellent high-quality dog foods on the market today. There is an even greater number of inferior products trying to capture your attention (and dog food dollars). As with finding the right Pomeranian for you, the adage, "You get what you pay for!" relates just as well to dog food. If you will take time to learn some basic facts about dog foods, you'll ultimately save money while providing a high-quality, balanced diet for your Pom.

The first thing to learn is how to read a dog food label. Look at the list of ingredients. These ingredients are listed by rank of percentage each represents of the total product. For example, if "chicken, corn, rice . . . " are listed as the first three ingredients in a particular dog food, then chicken is the largest single ingredient in the food, with corn being the next highest in percentage and rice being the third highest, and so forth, down the list of ingredients.

Normally, the first three or four items will combine to make up as much as 85 percent of the dog food, with the long list of additional ingredients making up the remaining 15 percent. Some companies play games with their ingredient lists by breaking down some items into several separate listings in order to change the percentage these appear to have in the list of ingredients. A dog food might truly have corn as its main ingredient with chicken next in line and someone in marketing might decide that a poultry-based food might be easier to market. Look out for foods that do this to make their product look different than it really is. The really high-quality or "premium" dog foods don't resort to this tactic.

Feeding Your Pomeranian

Another thing to read on the label is the maker's recommended feeding amounts for a dog the size of your Pom. Generally, these are broad brush recommendations and may or may not fit your dog. You will, possibly with your veterinarian's help, soon learn the best amount to feed your Pomeranian.

The better dog foods will have a toll-free telephone number that you can use to inquire about their products. Use this number! Find a company that will let you talk to a pet nutritionist or staff veterinarian. Ask questions about the food and about any Pomeranian test information they may have. Most of the better companies welcome questions and have skillful staff members available to help you with your dog food questions.

Premium dog food will not generally be available in grocery stores. It is usually available from veterinarians, pet stores, through better general feed stores, or some groomers. For your Pomeranian, premium quality dog food may be a little more expensive but it will be well worth it in terms of better health for your dog.

Commercial dog foods are generally in three forms: dry, semimoist, and canned.

Dry

There are a number of advantages to a high-quality dry dog food. Most importantly, there are several dry foods which can truthfully call themselves "nutritionally complete." As such they will be the balanced diet you are seeking. Additionally, a quality dry dog food will help clean your dog's teeth and gums. Dry dog food is the most economical way to feed a premium dog food. It is easy to feed, easy to store with no refrigeration needed to keep it fresh. Premium dry dog foods are high in palatability and digestibility producing smaller and firmer stools. Your dog actually eats less and gets more from a premium food. Dry dog

food has about 10 percent moisture, so be certain you keep plenty of clean, fresh water available to your Pom.

Semimoist

Semimoist food comes in burgers or in other shaped versions. It is very palatable and convenient. It is generally more expensive than dry food and contains approximately 30 percent moisture. Stools are usually less firm with semimoist dog food than with dry dog food.

Canned

Canned food is the most expensive dog food. It is quite palatable, but due to its high water content (approximately 75 percent) it can quickly spoil, even at room temperature. A tendency exists among dogs who are fed canned food to overeat which can lead to obesity and other problems. Stools are not firm with canned food and some foods produce particularly smelly excretions.

Homemade Diets

Unless you are a trained animal nutritionist with access to all the foods that will be needed for a balanced diet, this approach is best left alone. Your Pom will need a complete nutrition program and such a program is available in high-quality dog food from several companies that have spent multimillions to make it available to you for your Pomeranian.

Treats

Leave table scraps off your Pomeranian's menu. Don't start the habit of feeding the dog items from your plate and begging can be avoided. Also, table scraps aren't part of your goal—a nutritionally complete and balanced diet. A dog will often neglect its regular food in favor of treats and scraps.

There are some excellent dog biscuits available that are nutritionally complete and have the added bonus of helping to clean your dog's teeth and gums and give it a nutritional "chew" at the same time. Treats need to be apportioned with care lest they unbalance the balanced diet you are trying to maintain.

If you feed a high-quality dry dog food there is one trick you can use to give your pet a treat and some variety without throwing off the balanced diet. Put a small amount of your Pom's dry food in a microwave safe bowl. Add a teaspoon or two of water to the dry food. Microwave on high for about 30 seconds and allow the food to cool. The nutrients remain the same, but the fats in the dry food are pulled toward the surface. This will give the Pom the same food with a little different taste (not unlike the difference in a charcoal-broiled hamburger and one cooked on the stove). Don't use too much water on the dry dog food or you'll mess up stool firmness. This method, with a little more water, is helpful in feeding older dogs with teeth problems where a softer diet is needed.

Feeding Puppies (1 Year Old and Younger)

In order to get your puppy off to the best start possible, you will need a nutritionally complete balanced diet designed specifically for the needs of growing puppies. Puppies generally need twice as much in the way of nutrition than do adult dogs. Feed it the best high-quality puppy food available and you shouldn't run into any problems. But the key is starting the Pomeranian puppy out nutritionally right from the very beginning. Try to find a puppy diet, if you are changing, in a size that will be easily handled by a small-breed puppy like the Pomeranian. Several premium dry foods fit this requirement. A puppy under 6-months old should be fed three or four times daily. At six months cut back to two or

three times daily (depending on the individual needs of the dog).

Feeding Adult Dogs (Over 1 Year Old)

When your Pomeranian reaches physical maturity at around 1 year of age, its nutritional needs will change from those of a growing puppy into those of an adult. Two feedings per day will generally suffice as your Pom achieves its mature weight. Other than with added activities like breeding, showing, or obedience work, your Pom's nutritional needs should remain fairly constant for the next six or seven years. Of course, spaying or neutering your pet will change its nutritional requirements to more like those of an older dog.

Feeding Older Dogs (8 Years Old and Older)

When your Pom gets older its metabolic rate will slow down and it will need less energy, thus less fat and protein. The need of the older Pomeranian not to gain too much weight is never more apparent than at this point. (This is also true of the spayed or neutered Pom even before it has reached 8 years of age.)

One of the hardest things to convince dog owners of is that an older dog doesn't need the same amount of food it did when it was younger. "But Buffy always gets two cups of dog food," is the commonly heard reply when food reduction is suggested. It is sad, but true that Buffy's owner is not helping her live a long and healthy life by continuing to feed the same amount she ate when she was much younger.

Many of the premium dog foods now have foods designed for the less active metabolism of older dogs or for spayed and neutered dogs. Contact your veterinarian or the company that

Feeding Your Pomeranian

makes the dog food you have been using. (This would be a good time to take advantage of the 800 number of your premium dog food company.)

Finding a balanced diet for your Pomeranian that it likes isn't that difficult. Perhaps you can find a veterinarian that has taken a special interest in canine nutrition. Become a label-reader and ask lots of questions of the dog food companies. An aware consumer is a good consumer and your efforts will pay off for you and your Pomeranian.

Always consult with your veterinarian on special dietetic problems that afflict some dogs, but a good balanced diet program from puppyhood on should help your Pom avoid many ailments. Find a high-quality food and stick with it. If the product isn't doing what you think it should, follow this simple feeding trial:

Always compare apples to apples. Don't put a canned or semimoist food up against a dry food, for example. Obtain one sample of a new food that you believe might give you the results you desire. Put it in a dog dish near your pet's regular food. If the dog shows interest in the new food, let it eat an amount the equivalent to the regular amount you normally feed. Your dog may eat some of each or spurn the new food altogether. Don't let a piggish Pom eat more than it should regularly have.

If your dog likes the new food, follow the gradual-shift practice of mixing the old with the new until the new food is in place. Monitor stool firmness and volume, coat and skin condition and the overall appearance of your pet. If the new food passes all the tests after a month or so of trial, you may have found a product to stay with.

Don't be constantly seeking to change foods. If your current premium food is doing all the things you want with regard to stools, hair, skin, and so on, stay with it. Change your premium food when conditions dictate a change is needed. Don't change because you like another food's bag color, its ads on TV, or its lowered sale price, or change foods because your neighbor did. The food your pet eats is crucial to its well-being and should not be casually changed as one might change brands of gasoline.

If you do change to a premium food and there is some hesitation on your Pom's part in continuing to eat it, give the food a chance. Feed the new food in your usual manner. If the dog does not eat it, remove the food until the next regular feeding and give nothing else. Missing one feeding won't hurt most adult Pomeranians and once a dog starts to eat a food, it begins to like it. Your dog will normally eat less of a premium food because it takes less of this food to meet the dog's nutritional needs (this will also make the best premium food more economical in the long run than any cheap, bargain brand).

The food bowl is one good health indicator. Pay attention to the dog's eating habits. You may get an early warning to some ailment or physical condition that needs your veterinarian's attention. Also pay attention to the dog's bowel movements—another good health indicator.

Food Allergies

Some dogs will develop allergic reactions to some foods. Your veterinarian can help you recognize such allergies, isolate the cause, and find a diet that your dog's system can handle.

Grooming and Your Pomeranian

Grooming and the Pom—An Overview

The Pomeranian is not a difficult dog to keep well-groomed, but there are certain coat considerations that must be taken into account. Even though the Pom is a toy breed, its ancestry is northern. The Pomeranian, according to AKC Standard should have a coat of the following description:

Double coated, a short, soft, thick undercoat, with longer, coarse glistening outer coat consisting of guard hairs which must be harsh to the touch in order to give the proper texture for the coat to form a frill of profuse, standing-off straight hairs.

There are almost as many opinions about Pomeranian grooming as there are Pomeranian breeders, but one thing is very clear. The exacting requirements for a show dog are different than the needs of the average dog owner who has a Pom for a pet.

Grooming and Show Poms

A show Pomeranian will require an excellent coat tended in a careful, consistent manner. If you are serious about pursuing a show career for your Pom the most direct course will be the wisest. You have, of course, purchased a puppy from the best show stock available from the best available breeder. Go to this breeder and ask questions about show grooming. If this is not possible, find the Pomeranian exhibitor whose dogs evidence the best coats and the best show preparation. Pay this person whatever they ask for lessons on how to do what they do to make a Pomeranian show ready. Listen, learn, and follow their advice. But also remember, if exhibiting your Pomeranian is your goal, then no amount of external preparation can put a good coat on a dog whose breeding hasn't put the potential there for a good coat.

Grooming and Pet Poms

For the pet Pom owner, grooming holds no great mystery. Grooming tools for a Pomeranian consist of a good brush with natural bristles and a fine slicker brush or comb for the head, ear, and skirts. About once a day or so, gently brush your Pomeranian to keep its coat looking good. Brush away, or against the lay of the coat. Follow up with fine tooth comb on skirts and neck.

Regular brushing of a Pomeranian will keep the dog looking its best. Always brush away, or against the lay of the coat.

Use of a Groomer

About once a month (as included in the Pom budget previously mentioned) take your Pomeranian to a good, professional dog groomer. Depending on your dog's special needs, a bath, a flea dip or both may or may not be needed. The groomer will know how to keep your Pomeranian looking good. The groomer will also attend to hair trimming in the neck, feet, anus and anal gland, and will keep the toenails at an appropriate length. If you find that you enjoy grooming your own Pom (which many pet owners do not) learn what you must do and be consistent about it. Every exhibitor should certainly know how to show-groom their own dog but, for a pet

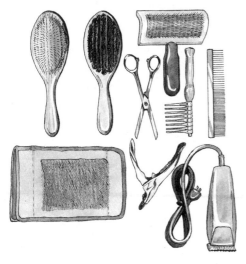

The basic grooming tools needed to keep a Pomeranian's coat in good condition are wire and bristle brushes, a wire slicker, a comb with medium and fine teeth, a tangle remover, nail clippers, an electric clipper, and a grooming glove.

owner, the monthly grooming session is usually done by a professional groomer. If you don't know a respected groomer, ask your veterinarian or pet shop to recommend one.

Using a professional groomer on a monthly basis will pay off in other than grooming re-

lated areas. A groomer can spot parasite problems, skin conditions, and other concerns that you might miss at home. Your groomer, along with your regular veterinarian, will join in making a team to keep things pleasant and healthy for your Pomeranian's teeth, ears, eyes, and nails. A good groomer can be a great aid to you in caring for your Pomeranian. Take time to find the best possible groomer, and encourage an active interest in your Pom. Take the groomer's advice as that of a professional who wants the best for your pet.

Regular visits to the groomer (who may be affiliated with a veterinarian, a quality pet shop, or a grooming shop) will also serve two other good purposes. First, your Pomeranian will like to get out and see new things. This is a good opportunity for a trip with a purpose. Secondly, it will be good for you to be out with your Pom with a chance to see new dog care products, toys, or other items that may interest you. You can also take some pride in your Pomeranian and of the care you have provided. A little showing-off never hurts.

Start Early

As with most other aspects of the Pomeranian, an early introduction to brushing and grooming is best for the Pom puppy. Thus your dog will not fear or loathe grooming and brushing. Begin as soon as possible to help your puppy learn that the daily brushing can be a pleasant time for both of you.

As a young puppy, take your Pom to your chosen groomer and introduce it to not only the groomer but to the sights, sounds, and smells of the place. Groomers will often take time to place a clipper next to a puppy, let it feel the warmth and vibration while being gently held. This works wonders in helping avoid fear later on.

Grooming and Your Pomeranian

Keeping Your Pom Presentable

Another useful technique that many Pomeranian owners use is the partial bath that can be given a couple times a week. Using a warm, damp wash cloth, wash the underside of your dog and make sure that no fecal material has adhered to the hair around the anus. (This is especially useful in keeping urine smell off the penis and surrounding area of your male Pomeranian.) With the regular care of a good professional groomer, your frequent brushing, and your touch-up cleaning a couple of times a week, your Pomeranian will stay in presentable shape. You will want your dog to look good.

Pom Coat Phases

It is important to know that all Poms go through phases when their coats are not at their best. The fluffy puppy you bought at 7 or 8 weeks of age will usually begin to radically shed its coat when it is about 4 months old and the coat will look fairly ragged.

The adult coat will begin to show up at about 6 months of age, as will evidence of the pup's adult color. The adult coat may hold on up to about a year when normally your Pom will shed its coat and look ragged again. This is especially true of male Poms. Females tend to shed in conjunction with their coming into season. Brood bitches with puppies also tend to lose their coats (a point to remember when looking at the mother of your prospective puppy, she may not look as good as she normally does).

Regular brushing will keep these shedding periods easier to manage. A puppy that has been taught to enjoy the regular brushing sessions will not be difficult to handle when shedding makes brushing all the more important.

Raising Quality Pomeranians

Reasons, Realities, and Responsibilities

As you have probably guessed by now, breeding Pomeranians (or any other breed for that matter) is not a recommended practice for even many experienced dog people, much less a beginner. However, you may very well be a "breeder-in-waiting," so some aspects of proper Pom production should be addressed.

The same kind of self-searching introspection that is required before you buy a Pomeranian is thrice needed before you decide to be a breeder of Pomeranians. A good question to ask is "Why do I want to raise Pomeranians?" If your answer to this question is to let your bitch have the experience of having puppies, save her some trouble. Many Pomeranian bitches have real difficulty in whelping and caesarean sections are commonly needed. Some little females are too small ever to successfully produce a litter of puppies and can die trying.

If your answer is motivated by some imagined pot of gold at the end of a Pomeranian rainbow, forget it. For every person who makes a dollar raising dogs, there are thousands who spend thousands in the same pursuit. Moreover, unless you are out of touch with the real world, you know that there are many more puppies born than there are responsible owners to care for them. Why add to the problem?

Another point to ponder before embarking on a breeding enterprise is this: Are you willing to take responsibility for any and all puppies you cause to be born and for their *entire* lives? They didn't ask to be brought in the world, you did it. You must own up to it. It is not uncommon for dog breeders to sell (or give) a good puppy to an apparently wonderful home only to have that puppy live a life of unmitigated hell that will require it to be reclaimed and placed in another home, or sometimes even mercifully be put to sleep. Breeders go through that experience far too often.

If raising Poms is a sort of status thing based on some personal ego-bolstering need, buy a really good Pomeranian puppy and campaign it to an AKC Championship or to an obedience ring degree. That's where the status is with dogs, and you'll even have some fun doing it (if your ego can stand any little setbacks you may encounter).

If, after falling in love with Pomeranians, you feel that you would like to make a serious effort to improve the breed, then you may have some basis to consider becoming a Pomeranian breeder. Talk to the breeders you've met. Meet others. Listen to them. Read and study all you can about canine genetics and dog breeding. Read the Pomeranian standard until you can quote it line for line. Examine your bankbook and then rethink the whole deal. If you still want to breed Poms, start small with a clear understanding of the pedigrees, genetics, and possible problems involved.

Striving to produce better and better dogs is not an easy undertaking. Meet as many dog breeders as you can. Listen to their stories of failure and success, or achievement and sacrifice before you give serious thought to joining their ranks. The pursuit of excellence (the only valid reason to breed dogs) is not without its costs.

The Female Estrous Cycle

A female Pomeranian will normally come into season (or estrous) approximately every six months. Generally, she will "come into heat" the first time when she is between 6- and 8-months old. You will recognize the onset of estrous by the swelling of the vulva combined with blood-tinged vaginal discharge. This

Raising Quality Pomeranians

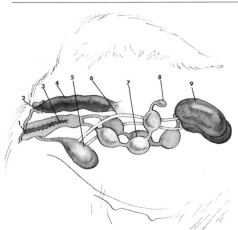

The reproductive system of a female Pomeranian:
1. vulva 2. anus 3. vagina 4. rectum 5. bladder
6. ureter 7. developing embryo 8. ovaries 9. kidneys

phase lasts seven to ten days. Males will be drawn to her throughout this time, but she will not be ready to receive them (nor can she conceive) because ovulation has not yet occurred.

The fertile phase of the estrous cycle comes with ovulation, occurs around the ninth day and means your Pom's eggs (ova) are ready to be fertilized. At this time she will accept a male and allow him to mount (mate) her. This fertile phase can last as long as seven days. Vaginal discharge will subside somewhat and the blood color will turn clear. If your Pomeranian bitch is not impregnated, the ova will lose their viability (ability to be fertilized) and she will be out of heat until the process starts again in about five and a half months. Your bitch should normally not be allowed to become pregnant until her third heat at between 18 to 20 months of age.

The Stud

As with so many other aspects of the Pomeranian, the search for a sire (or stud dog)

should begin well in advance of the projected mating time. Wisely you have studied the pedigrees of your dam and of several potential sires. After careful consideration and consultation with seasoned breeders, one hopes you have chosen a male that will blend his genetic qualities with those of your female and that possesses no open (overt) or hidden (covert) defects or flaws that he can pass on to the puppies. This stud dog should be at least 1 year old and since your female is a virgin, it would be good, when possible, if the male has been used as a stud dog before. Usually the male will breed better at home, therefore the female generally goes to him.

You should have your female (and the stud as well) checked by a veterinarian for the presence of a venereally transmitted bacterial disease known as brucellosis, which can wreak havoc with breeding specimens (sometimes causing aborted litters or sterility). Most serious breeders will require a brucellosis-free statement about your bitch from a vet.

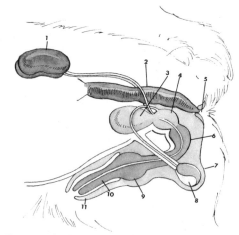

The reproductive system of a male Pomeranian:
1. kidneys 2. rectum 3. bladder 4. prostate 5. anus
6. urethra 7. scrotum 8. testes 9. bulb 10. penis
11. sheath

Raising Quality Pomeranians

You would be wise to have the stud fee (payment for the male's mating with your female) clearly spelled out in writing. Most stud dog owners will want a set fee or their pick of the puppies as payment. Since most Pomeranian litters are very small (one to three puppies) and the pick of the litter might be the only show prospect (if you have even one), the straight payment of the fee may be best for you. You will also want to have an arrangement for another mating if your female fails to conceive after the mating. Usually the owner of the stud dog will guarantee that your bitch will conceive or she can be mated again to the same male at her next heat.

You may want to be on-site when the mating takes place. If you do not know the stud dog owner well, you want to be sure that the exact Pomeranian male you want as the sire of your puppies is the one doing the servicing.

If your Pomeranian is not an excellent, show-quality specimen, the stud dog owner may refuse to let your female be mated to his or her male. This is a good attitude for a stud dog owner to take. If your female is likely to produce poor quality puppies, the desirability of the stud dog as a breeder can be lessened. The better your female, the better chances for producing that outstanding puppy that will enhance the demand for the stud dog. This makes starting with the very best all the more important.

Mating

Since you have been considering this mating for many months in advance you will have your female in good health prior to the onset of the estrous cycle. She should have your veterinarian's approval before you breed her and have been wormed and be up to date on her vaccinations.

As mentioned, the ovulating phase of the estrous cycle is when your female can be mounted. Breeders generally try to schedule the mating (or matings) on the ninth and twelfth days after onset of heat.

Give the male and the female Pomeranians a chance to get used to one another before the mating. If possible, use a previously bred male for your female's first mating.

Oversee the actual mating to prevent any injury to either dog. Be sure to keep the female away from any other males even after mating has taken place.

Raising Quality Pomeranians

When copulating, the male and female may be "tied" or locked together by the action of the penis and vagina. This is a natural manifestation and will cease when the mating urges subside. Your female can become tied with the stud dog more than once during the two or so days of maximum receptibility (or she may mate with another dog after the initial mating has taken place so keep her from other males until after estrous has ended!).

False Pregnancy

Some non-pregnant Pomeranian females will show all the outward signs of pregnancy. This will sometimes even happen to the tiny, "teacup" Poms to whom normal pregnancy and whelping would be impossible. Hormonal abnormality rather than exposure to a male can bring on this reaction. Sometimes false pregnancy is not just a harmless condition. It can be an indicator of pyometritis, which can result in sterility or may require an ovariohysterectomy. Consult your veterinarian if false pregnancy occurs.

Some little Pom females have adopted other female's puppies or even kittens (or have treated a favorite toy like a puppy) during the seven or eight weeks this condition lasts.

Pregnancy

The regular gestation period for an impregnated bitch will be approximately 63 days after the mating but generally a little less for Pomeranians. At about six weeks of the nine-week period she will begin to show pregnancy with her abdomen becoming larger and her teats becoming enlarged.

Your Pomeranian dam will need tender loving care during this time, especially if it is her first litter. You should have been feeding her a nutritionally complete diet and she should be heavy with pups not heavy with excess fat. Her exercise need not be eliminated, but should not be strenuous. You should separate her from other dogs during the last couple of weeks before the puppies are born. You should alert the children not to pick her up and she should have her "den" nearby for her emotional well-being.

The Whelping Box

Introduce the dam to the whelping box which is a box tall enough where she won't be jumping in and out, yet large enough for her to have plenty of space. The box needs to be in a quiet place where your Pom feels comfortable. Encourage her to use the whelping box for dozing and at night just prior to delivery day. (Make sure you have safe bedding that will not allow a tiny puppy to be smothered down in some folds somewhere.) Her comfort and relaxation are crucial prior to actual whelping.

Preparations for Whelping

Some Pom breeders have the area trimmed of hair around her nipples and her vulva; others reject the idea. Any long hair on her back legs that could wrap around and strangle a puppy should definitely be removed. As whelping time approaches she may become restless and ill at ease. She may stop eating as the time nears. She will fuss with the bedding in the whelping box. Keep her quiet and as comfortable as possible.

Like Queen Victoria a hundred years ago, most Pomeranian owners are devoted to the breed and remain Pom people for life. ▶

44

Raising Quality Pomeranians

Whelping

While dogs have been having puppies without your help for thousands of years, your Pomeranian will need your rapt attention, especially if this is her first litter. If you are the least bit unsure about this whole experience or this is your first job as a birthing attendant, you would do well to move your bitch and her whelping box to the veterinarian's office before she gets too close to whelping time. You might also get an experienced breeder (someone your Pom likes) to help you.

Pomeranians normally are good mothers and are very attentive to their puppies. Pomeranian litters are usually quite small with three puppies being considered a large litter.

If your Pomeranian dam is a show prospect (as she probably should be if you have decided to breed her) she will be close to the small size required for a show dog. Her size and the compact body of a show quality Pom bring a real possibility of birthing problems. You need

◀ Pomeranians come in a variety of solid and particolors to match most anyone's preference. Underneath each color is the same "little big dog" that has so many fans the world over.

to be prepared, should they occur. If your bitch has labored strenuously for more than two hours without success, a caesarean may be necessary to save her life or to save the lives of the puppies. You should have your veterinarian on call.

The possibility of birthing problems is one consideration you should take into account when you decide to breed Pomeranians. If you have little or no experience in this area, by all means use your veterinarian.

Given an uncomplicated delivery, the mother should pull away the placenta as soon as the puppy is born. She should begin nosing, licking, and cleaning the puppy. It is this action, the nudging and licking, that actually stimulates the new puppy to begin breathing. Pom puppies are truly tiny, weighing between 3 to 5 ounces (85–142 g) with some as small as 1 ounce (28 g) on record!

Your Pom female usually will eat the afterbirth, thus severing the umbilical cord. If she fails to pull away the placental membranes and free the puppy from the sac where it has been nurtured while in the womb, you should move in immediately to help her. After you clean away the membranes, clear the puppy's airway of any mucous fluid. Rub the puppy gently with a towel or wash cloth simulating the mother's licking and nuzzling.

If no immediate problems exist, take the mother Pom and her puppies to the veterinarian to assess the health of both mother and puppies and ascertain if she has sufficient colostrum-rich mother's milk—to get them off to a good start and to feed them. If your puppies have dewclaws they can be removed at this time.

Care of the Puppies

Your puppies must be kept warm and get enough milk. A healthy puppy will feel warm, sleep a lot, and seldom whimper. Be alerted

Raising Quality Pomeranians

if your puppies don't fit that picture. Constant whimpering, restlessness, and low temperature or body weight can signal feeding problems. Your bitch may not be producing enough milk, or there may be some other difficulty.

Under normal conditions puppies grow and develop quickly. Generally, you will have three or less puppies so you can easily monitor their progress (imagine what your efforts would have to be if you had one of the larger breeds whose litters can number a dozen or more). If your Pomeranian bitch will not or cannot feed her puppies, you will have to do so. The puppies will need a warm place and be kept between 85 to 90° F (29–32° C) for the first 14 days. The temperature can be gradually decreased to 75° F (24° C) by their first month of age. Both overheating and chilling can be harmful to the puppies. Use a regular weather thermometer in good working condition to monitor their environment.

For handfeeding your puppies, follow your veterinarian's recommendations as to what milk replacement to use (Esbilac is one brand name) and how to feed. Remember that Pom puppies are tiny at birth. Use an eye dropper or one of the bottles developed to feed small animals (available from your veterinarian or pet store). Warm the milk to between 95 and 100° F (35–38° C). Feed the puppies as much as they will eat. A good indicator is the absence of whimpering and presence of fat, little full bellies. A newborn puppy should be fed about every four hours on a regular basis. As they grow, you will be able to lengthen the period between feeding. Follow your veterinarian's advice on this.

Normally your little Pomeranian female will be a good mother and, barring birthing problems brought on by her small size, she should be able to do the job nicely. Keep her in a quiet area. Limit noise and unnecessary visitors and feed her as much of her regular, nutritionally complete diet as she wants to eat. You can supplement her diet, if your veterinarian advises it.

Remember that she will look pretty shopworn with an almost certain loss of coat during her puppy production. You will be interested in her puppies to be sure, but remember to be gentle and reassuring with her, especially on the first litter. Remember to give her praise and not just ooh-and-ah over her puppies.

Weaning the puppies can begin anywhere from four to six weeks after birth. You can assist your Pom mother by moistening some premium quality puppy food and interesting the puppies in their new food form. Let them taste the food on your fingers and gradually introduce them to it under controlled circumstances.

Don't leave food or water in the whelping box. Remember that even a relatively shallow drinking bowl can be deep enough to drown a small, uncoordinated Pomeranian puppy. As your puppies begin to eat more and more of the puppy food, decrease the food to the mother. Her milk supply will gradually subside.

Socializing the Puppies

You must now fill the position of assistant socializer of the puppies. You have followed the veterinarian's advice so mother and puppies are all healthy. You and the mother dog have seen the puppies through their early growth stages, from the time when they were blind and helpless, dependent totally on you and her. You have watched them grow, open their eyes, take clumsy steps, and identify you as their friend. You have handled them on a regular basis and have done so gently. They are now active, little balls of fur competing for care and attention. They will have their own pecking order even in a small litter. You will have learned much of canine behavior by watching their actions now. You have supplied the puppies with lots of human contact, kept them in a safe environment, and helped them learn the first lessons that will bring them full circle to the time when they, like the puppy you chose at the start of this adventure, are ready to learn how to be responsible adult Pomeranians.

Your responsibilities now are similar to those you had when you brought your puppy home. You must see the puppies are safe and comfortable. You should have some good help in this from the mother dog. She will have given them some valuable early lessons in what is expected of them.

You are now in the reverse position of when you were seeking a Pom puppy. You now have puppies that will need loving, responsible care. You will now face the quandary that so many breeders experience: "Now that we've got them, what do we do with them?" Remember that you are responsible for these puppies being alive and that while they are alive, the responsibility for their ultimate well-being is yours.

Breeding Approaches

There are as many approaches to breeding Pomeranians as there are Pomeranian breeders. Choosing which line or stud dog will help you achieve the ideal you are seeking tends to be a matter of personal conviction. There are, however, three primary approaches that dog breeders (and other animal breeders) take: inbreeding, linebreeding, and outcrossing.

Inbreeding

Inbreeding is the mating of close relatives, brothers and sisters, fathers and daughters, mothers and sons. The purpose of inbreeding is to intensify the genetic makeup of these close relatives in their offspring. The hope is that the good qualities will become that much stronger and easier to pass on to coming generations.

This is called "fixing type." This means that you would have a line (or family) in which there would be no bad qualities sneaking in to mess up your plans for that perfect Pom. It is true that inbreeding has the capability of fixing type on the good attributes. There is however another side to inbreeding.

Inbreeding is just an approach, not an automatic way to perfection. If inbreeding can intensify the good it can also intensify the bad. Because of this double-edged sword that cuts both ways in the none-too-apparent world of dog genetics, inbreeding is best left to the experts.

Linebreeding

Linebreeding is again the mating of related dogs, but not close relatives as in inbreeding. Nephew to aunt, niece to uncle, cousin to cousin are examples of linebreeding. The goal is the same as inbreeding. Linebreeders hope to build up the good genes while cutting down on the bad genes.

It is because of the distance between these relatives that linebreeding is somewhat slower than inbreeding in achieving success. But again, linebreeding is also much slower in causing failure.

Outcrossing

In the strictest sense of the word, outcrossing would be the mating of dogs of totally dissimilar breeds (a Pom and a Pug for example). This is actually called crossbreeding. Outcrossing would be taking a Pomeranian from a famous English family of Poms and breeding it to a member of a famous American family of Poms which have no close common ancestry to the English family in any generation. The outcross might do well or what breeders call "nick." They would say that the English dog nicked with the American dog. This would mean, at least for the first generation, that the specimens would be quite good, perhaps better than either parent.

The goal of inbreeding and linebreeding is to limit the number of genes (and hence the amount of difference) in the family or "strain." The purpose of outbreeding is to introduce new genes possibly in an attempt to correct some condition in the strain. For example, Pom Strain A has excellent size, type (shape), and color, but the coat quality leaves much to be desired. You, as the Pom breeder, have studied other strains (B, C, D, E, etc.) and have decided that Strain B would be a likely source of new genetic material in your dogs. You chose B because even though this strain has some weaknesses in size and other areas, it produces superb coats. The ultimate goal of this outcross is to produce offspring that will retain the good A qualities of size, type, and color *combined* with the excellent coat qualities of B. You may reach that goal on the first cross, but then again you may not. You may end up with puppies that have all the coat qualities of A (weak at best) with the size, type, and color of B (also weak). Since this was a pure outcross you may have, if you breed this long enough, every range in each quality from very bad to very good.

Outcrossing, like inbreeding, is best left to the pros. If you decide to breed Poms, take your time and follow the lead of the more experienced breeders that you have met.

Your Pomeranian and Medical Care

Keeping Your Pom Healthy

Preventing health problems is far less costly (and far less painful) than treating health problems. By creating a healthy environment and by having a preventive orientation you can accomplish much in the way of keeping injuries, maladies, and other unhealthy conditions away from your Pomeranian. You already know about the possible health hazards posed to the Pomeranian by small children and big dogs. You already know about puppy-proofing your home. You already know about the potential bone-breaking that can come from even moderate jumping, falls, or misdirected human feet.

Here is some additional information you can add to your stock of knowledge. Armed with the ways to stop problems before they occur, you are on your way to keeping your Pom as healthy as possible for as long as it lives.

Medical Care Team

Your Pomeranian will need to have a team of concerned humans to make its good health the rule rather than the exception. On this team you will have yourself, the other members of your household, your Pom's groomer, and foremost, your Pom's veterinarian.

You and your family have already learned some accident prevention ideas. You need to learn about the most common diseases, parasites, and medical conditions that may confront your dog. You need to know how to recognize these health enemies.

Your Pom's groomer is in an excellent position to monitor several aspects of your dog's health. Not only does a skilled, professional groomer bring a good deal of expertise and experience to your team, he or she also sees your dog often enough to know a lot about it

and rarely enough to notice any subtle changes that may be too gradual to be easily spotted by you and your family who see the Pomeranian every day. Make it a point to let the groomer know that his or her opinion is respected and requested in matters concerning the health of your Pom.

The key member of this health team is, of course, your veterinarian. Nobody is better trained or more knowledgeable in how to keep your Pomeranian healthy than is your dog's regular veterinarian. The best use of a veterinarian is not just in an emergency, but as a caring professional who sees your pet on regular visits. Take time to establish a good rapport with this key team member. The veterinarian's skill and knowledge will be vital from your dog's puppyhood to its old age.

Strive for good, clear communication with your Pom's veterinarian. He or she will need to know accurate information, without embellishment, to make an accurate diagnosis, and prescribe an effective treatment. Ask questions and make sure you understand the answers. Neither you nor the veterinarian can really help your Pomeranian with partial or inaccurate knowledge.

Find a good veterinarian and then follow his or her instructions—*to the letter*. You may have a great deal of knowledge about a great many things, but trust the medical care of your pet to the person with the best training—your veterinarian.

Preventive Care for Your Pomeranian

Your in-home health care and routine visits to the veterinarian provide the basis for continuing good health for your Pomeranian. The best veterinarian in the world can't help your dog if you don't take the dog to the veterinarian's office on a regular schedule.

Your Pomeranian and Medical Care

This schedule will include visits for check-ups and for vaccinations. Checkups will spot many potential health problems before they arise. Vaccinations will protect your Pomeranian from a number of diseases and infections. Having your Pom immunized against a number of diseases isn't just smart, in some places it's the law!

Vaccinations

Your puppy should have received its first immunizations while still under the breeder's care. The first shots include initial vaccinations for distemper, parvovirus, hepatitis, leptospirosis, parainfluenza, coronavirus, and bordetella. At 5 or 6 weeks of age your puppy should have gotten these shots. Follow-up shots will be necessary for most of these immunizations and your veterinarian will set up a schedule (usually needed at 8 to 10 weeks of age and again at 12 weeks).

Diseases Controlled by Vaccination

As your Pomeranian grows up it will need a rabies vaccination. Your dog will also require periodic rabies booster shots throughout its life.

Be sure your veterinarian has a complete record of all vaccinations (and other treatments) your puppy received before you got it. This is the beginning of your Pom's health record which should be kept up to date as long as the dog lives.

Distemper

Once the most deadly killer of puppies and young dogs, distemper is a disease that is both widespread and highly contagious. Distemper affects all the members of the canine family and a number of other small mammals. It was not uncommon, a number of years ago, for distemper to rage through a kennel and destroy most of the young dogs and all of the puppies.

As a viral disease, the onset of symptoms would rapidly appear about a week after exposure to an infected animal. At first, distemper would resemble a cold with a fever and a runny nose. The dog would then typically stop eating, appear tired and listless. Sometimes vomiting or diarrhea would be present and the skin leathers of the nose and pads of the feed would thicken, which promoted old time dog breeders to label distemper as hard pad disease.

Although some dogs would seem to recover, distemper would linger and later reappear in the form of convulsions, nervous twitching, paralysis, and death. Thankfully, vaccination has greatly decreased the incidence of this dreadful disease.

Rabies

Rabies or hydrophobia was the feared "madness" that occurred periodically since earliest time among dogs and other animals. The mere mention of the word can still conjure up terrible mental pictures of mad dogs, foaming at the mouth and running amok terrorizing a neighborhood.

Rabies is an acute infectious disease of warmblooded mammals (including man) transmitted most commonly by a bite. Skunks, raccoons, bats, and foxes are among the wild animals thought to be the most common carriers of rabies. The disease still affects populations of wild animals in some parts of the world, but has been effectively eradicated in England and other countries largely by the use of strict quarantine.

Because of the fatal nature of the disease, its frightening symptoms and the relative ease of transmission in earlier times, rabies joined the bubonic plague, leprosy, anthrax, and a few other so-called nightmare diseases that fell eventually thanks to medicine. Louis Pasteur in 1885 developed the first vaccine against rabies. His early work, crude by modern standards, set the stage for a number of other immunizations that have made rabies a rare disease among humans (about one case a year in the United States) but a disease that should be vaccinated against in every dog.

Leptospirosis

Leptospirosis is another canine disease that can be transmitted by humans. This bacterial disease is most commonly spread by exposure to an animal with leptospirosis or by ingestion of water that has been polluted by the urine of an infected animal.

You can recognize leptospirosis by a loss of appetite, fever, vomiting, and diarrhea. In advanced cases, serious damage to the liver and kidneys can result. Jaundice, weak hind quarters, sores in the soft tissue in the mouth, and abdominal pain are also symptoms that dogs infected with leptospirosis might evidence.

Parvovirus

The parvovirus attacks the intestines of dogs. It causes a viral infection than can spell death for many unvaccinated or untreated dogs at any time, but especially affects puppies under 4 months of age.

Listlessness and loss of appetite, followed by vomiting as well as heavy, sometimes bloody diarrhea, are classic parvovirus symptoms. Infected puppies will suffer from extreme dehydration. Unless prompt veterinary care is sought, death will often be the outcome. If medical care is given to offset the effects of the dehydration and to handle any secondary infections, there is a reasonable chance of survival.

Parvovirus can be controlled by vaccination and common sense. Any unvaccinated dog should be viewed as a potential victim. If your Pom is not vaccinated and should encounter a dog infected with parvovirus on the street during your walks, you could be inviting this dangerous virus to attack your dog.

Hepatitis

Infectious canine hepatitis can affect a dog of any age. The severity of the disease can range from a relatively light ailment to a death-dealing viral infection which can cause some dogs to die in less than a day after first observance of the symptoms.

The symptoms of hepatitis are: listlessness, fever, tonsillitis, abdominal pain, vomiting, and hemorrhaging.

Parainfluenza

Commonly miscalled kennel cough, parainfluenza is a highly contagious viral disease. Parainfluenza can spread quickly through dogs that are kept near to one another (as in a kennel, but certainly not limited to kennels). Parainfluenza brings on tracheobronchitis which is characterized by a dry hacking cough followed by retching to expel throat mucus.

Parainfluenza, in and of itself is not that debilitating. Untreated, however, this so-called kennel cough can leave a dog wide open to more severe respiratory ailments and secondary infections. As with the other preventable diseases, parainfluenza should be prevented by vaccination. Good treatment for tracheobronchitis is best provided by a veterinarian with the patient kept away from other dogs to lessen the contagion.

Coronavirus

Coronavirus is another highly contagious malady affecting unvaccinated dogs of all ages. Coronavirus looks very much like parvovirus.

Your veterinarian will be able to distinguish one from the other.

Typically, coronavirus causes a severe diarrhea, often foul smelling, watery, and sometimes marked with blood. Regardless of the final diagnosis, parvovirus or coronavirus, if such symptoms are in evidence with your Pom, call your veterinarian and isolate the dog until you can take it to the animal hospital.

Bordetella

Bordetella is a bacterial infection often connected with tracheobronchitis. Your veterinarian will be able to prevent bordetella by an immunization which will strike at the whole range of the tracheobronchial infections.

Parasites

Internal Parasites

Worms are common in adult dogs and puppies and they can pose serious health problems. Your veterinarian can find out if worms are present in your Pomeranian and will prescribe the most appropriate treatment. Avoid treating your Pom with wormers available from a variety of retail sources. Also avoid any homemade worming preparations or recipes. The veterinarian has precise diagnostic tools to help identify the offending parasite and up-to-the-hour treatments to eradicate it. Trust him or her to do it right.

Regular checkups will catch most parasitic problems. Nevertheless, if at any time you suspect that your pet may have worms, don't wait. Take your Pomeranian to the veterinarian right away and make sure.

Worms are generally detected by microscopic examination of fecal material or of a blood sample. The most common worms infecting dogs are: roundworms, hookworms, tapeworms, and heartworms. Each of these

must be dealt with by a specific treatment from your veterinarian.

Roundworms: Roundworms are most often found in puppies, although dogs of any age can be infested. Puppies generally get roundworms even before they are born, if the mother dog has them.

Puppies who have roundworms will not thrive. Their appearance is often just not quite as sharp and shiny as uninfected puppies. They may have a pendulous abdomen ("potbelly"). They may also pass worms through their stools or when they vomit. Your veterinarian can handle the medical aspects of eliminating roundworms after making a stool examination first and an evaluation of the dog later.

Good housekeeping on your part will help eliminate these parasites. Keep the puppies' area extremely clean and sanitized, safely dispose of any and all stools promptly.

The flea, which plays a key role in the life cycle of the tapeworm, actually serves as an intermediate host for the tapeworm's eggs. When a dog swallows an infested flea the eggs mature in the dog's intestines. Tapeworm eggs can also be found in raw meat and fish.

Hookworms: Although hookworms will infect dogs of all ages, these blood suckers will really cause your puppies to do poorly. The puppies have bloody stools, inky stools, fail to maintain weight, and fail to eat properly. Since hookworms attach themselves to the small intestine and do suck blood, anemia can be the sometimes fatal result.

See your veterinarian quickly and keep your dogs away from infested areas and, as with roundworms, dispose of all stools as soon as possible.

Tapeworms: Fleas are a common transmitter of tapeworms. Though they rarely debilitate a dog, these flat, segmented parasites steal from your dog's health.

Your veterinarian can treat the dog and assist you in a plan to prevent the tapeworm's return. This parasite is just another good reason for eliminating fleas from your dog's environment.

Mosquitoes spread heartworm from infected dogs to uninfected dogs. The heartworm larvae mature in the dog's heart and cause great damage there.

Heartworms: This wide-ranging worm is transmitted to dogs by a mosquito. The mosquito, itself infested with the heartworm larvae, passes this larvae into a dog's bloodstream and ultimately to its heart.

Just because your Pomeranian is predominantly an inside dog, don't ignore the preventive treatment that can keep this fatal parasite from clogging your dog's heart. Your veterinarian can help you with medication that will prevent infestation. This medication will prevent the need for an expensive, possibly risky, and prolonged treatment and save your pet from an early and miserable death.

External Parasites

Fleas: Fleas are the bane of many a dog's existence. They are the most common external parasite afflicting dogs. They feed on your dog's blood and in extreme cases cause anemia. Generally they can make your Pomeranian miserable. Since many Poms live inside, fleas can make dog owners miserable too. Your dog can even become infected with tapeworms transmitted by fleas.

Some Pomeranians suffer from flea bite allergy. While fleas are bothersome to all dogs, dogs that are allergic to fleas suffer much more. Hair loss, skin problems, and incessant scratching may indicate this allergy. Prompt treatment by a veterinarian can do much to alleviate this uncomfortable condition.

Flea bite allergy is also another good reason for working diligently to eliminate fleas from your Pom's environment and to keep them out! Dealing with fleas involves a warfare mentality—a them-or-us kind of thinking. You have to hit fleas at *every* possible site in order to achieve even limited victory. Everywhere a dog infested with fleas has been will harbor fleas—the bed, the yard, the doghouse, the car, your house. If you fail to attack the fleas in *any* of these areas then you have failed—they will be back.

Your Pomeranian and Medical Care

Flea dips, flea shampoos, flea powder, flea collars, and flea sprays are all designed for on-dog use. Check with your veterinarian about these products and follow the manufacturer's instructions implicitly. Be sure to treat the Pom's "den" and its bedding. Flea foggers will provide some relief for your home. In severe cases you may need to call an exterminator. Fleas spend only about 10 percent of their time on the dog. That means that 90 percent of the time fleas are available to visit your home, yard, and so on.

There are yard sprays for the outside areas your Pomeranian uses. Again, be careful of their use and for more serious infestations consult a professional exterminator.

Regular monthly grooming by a professional will spot fleas before they get to the severe stage. But always remember you cannot beat a flea infestation by dealing with just part of the problem. The *entire* environment must be treated.

Ticks: Your Pomeranian can come in contact with another vicious blood sucker, the tick, on walks or while playing outside. Although regular dips will control ticks rather well, you need to know how to handle them if you see them.

Ticks are much larger than fleas and as they engorge on blood they can get as big as a marble if left in place. Never simply pull a tick off your dog. You will leave part of its mouth parts in the dog, which may cause infection. A good way to get them out cleanly is to place a drop of alcohol at the location where the tick is attached to the skin. Let the alcohol cause the tick to loosen its grip a bit. Using tweezers, grasp the tick as close to the dog's skin as possible and pull slowly. Be sure to get the mouth of the tick when you pull the pest away. Put alcohol on the bite and dispose of the tick carefully (they can get back on the dog or on you if simply dropped on the ground).

Ticks have gained recent notoriety with the discovery of Lyme disease in humans. This potentially life-threatening disease is transmitted by the deer tick and has been found in many areas across the United States. If a tick bites you, save it, and see a medical professional immediately to identify it.

Ear Mites: One parasite that can cause your Pomeranian great discomfort is the ear mite. These microscopic mites live in the ear canal. They cause the development of a dark waxy residue and can be easily transmitted to and from other dogs (or cats). Symptoms include head shaking and ear scratching. The veterinarian can identify and treat them quickly and effectively.

Mange: Another problem brought to the dog by mites is mange. There are two kinds: red mange (or demodectic) and scabies (or sarcoptic).

Red mange especially affects old dogs and young puppies and causes scruffy hair loss and other symptoms. It varies in degree of severity from dog to dog. Itching may sometimes accompany red mange. Seek help immediately. Don't mess around with mange.

Scabies mites burrow into the dog's epidermal skin layer. They are highly contagious and can spread from your dog to other dogs or to you. Sarcoptic mange causes unsightly hair loss and a lot of itching.

Your groomer may act as an early warning system here. See your veterinarian immediately for proper diagnosis and treatment.

Other Skin Problems: Like other dog breeds, Pomeranians are sometimes beset with any of a number of skin problems—allergies, fungi, and so on. Flea bite allergy is one skin problem that stems directly from an allergic reaction to fleas (see page 00). Some dogs may develop allergies to certain foods, or to some other aspect of their environments. Your veterinarian can usually pinpoint the sources of these conditions and help in either preventing the problem or in dealing with it.

It is good to recognize that some skin conditions may be of a genetic origin. Your dog's problem may be something that it inherited from its parents. This is just another good reason to take special care in choosing a Pomeranian puppy. Rely on your veterinarian in diagnosing and treating skin problems. Home remedies here can often make a condition much worse. Let a professional, with all the information and resources available, develop the treatment plan for your Pomeranian. You won't regret it—nor will your pet.

Common Illnesses and Medical Problems

Vomiting and Diarrhea

Some vomiting and diarrhea can result from normal factors, like dietetic changes, or

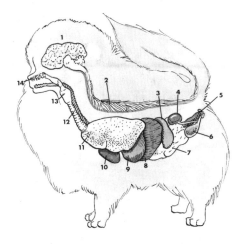

The major internal organs of the Pomeranian 1. brain 2. spinal cord 3. spleen 4. kidneys 5. rectum 6. bladder 7. intestine 8. stomach 9. liver 10. heart 11. lungs 12. trachea 13. larynx 14. nasal sinus

from stress, but in puppies are most commonly caused by intestinal parasites. Both vomiting and diarrhea are possible indicators of other more serious conditions. Any prolonged vomiting or diarrhea in your Pom deserves at least a call to the veterinarian's office. Early treatment is effective treatment. Until you have gained more experience, take care in all such situations.

If either vomiting or diarrhea becomes severe or continues for more than 12 to 24 hours, you would be wise to take your Pom to your veterinarian.

Constipation

If normal bowel movements have not been occurring for your Pom or if the dog is clearly straining to defecate, constipation may be the cause. Many dietetic causes, such as eating bones, or a sudden change in dog food can bring on constipation. Sometimes a Pom that has been traveling and has not been allowed relief-walks on a regular basis will become constipated.

Most constipation is a minor problem, but check with your veterinarian if it continues, especially if the dog is in obvious pain and crying out while trying to defecate.

Impacted Anal Glands

The anal glands lie just under the skin on each side of the anus. Normally these glands are emptied of their strong-smelling secretions during defecation. Sometimes, however, these glands become clogged (impacted) and must be emptied by hand. Some groomers will provide this service. Your veterinarian can also show you how to do this. When you see a Pomeranian scooting along the floor or ground, dragging its rear end, impacted anal glands or possible tapeworm irritation could be the cause.

Your Pomeranian and Medical Care

Emergency Care

Poisoning

Protecting your Pom puppy from some toxic products and conditions has been discussed. There are other accidental poisoning possibilities you should know about that will generally require immediate veterinary care.

Regular antifreeze is highly poisonous but has an odor and taste that attracts dogs. A number of indoor and yard plants are deadly if eaten. Chocolate can be poisonous to most dogs. Some insect bites or stings can cause strong allergic reactions in your Pomeranian.

Be alert to listlessness, convulsions, disoriented behavior, vomiting, diarrhea, and a change in the color of mucous membranes. Get your pet to the veterinarian as soon as possible when these symptoms appear.

Accidents

Many accidents can be prevented by just thinking ahead and being a little creatively paranoid about things that can hurt your Pom. But as careful as you are, accidents still happen.

If your Pomeranian has been injured, be careful not to make the injury worse or to be bitten by a dog in pain. Using a piece of cloth (a necktie or handkerchief will do) as a muzzle, gently lift your Pom and place it on a makeshift stretcher made of your shirt, a towel, or some other cloth that will allow you to move the injured dog without danger of further injury. Call your veterinarian's clinic to alert them to the situation and drive safely there.

Bleeding

If your Pomeranian appears to be bleeding, identify the source of the blood and apply firm, but gentle, pressure to the area. If the injury is on an extremity, place a tourniquet between the wound and the heart, but it must be loosened every 15 minutes. Continued bleeding or any significant blood loss, or a gaping wound will require veterinary attention. Treat any bleeding as a serious condition.

Heatstroke

A healthy, happy Pomeranian can be dying or dead in just a few minutes in a car with poor ventilation and high inside temperature. The double coat of the Pomeranian cannot insulate the dog in a closed space. Because Poms love to travel, they are subjected sometimes more often to this danger; one that is often ignored even by caring Pomeranian owners. Just a few minutes in the sun, even on a moderately warm day—60° F (15.6° C) or so—or even with some windows partially rolled down can mean the dog's death.

One Pom fancier was returning from a trip to the groomer when he was stopped by the police for a minor traffic violation. He was asked to step away from the car and approach the police car to get his ticket, have his license checked, and so forth. In just that short time, the Pom began to show heatstroke symptoms. Thanks to the police, now in an escort role, the dog was rushed to the veterinarian. Thus its life was saved. Never, never take chances by leaving your Pom in an enclosed area unattended. It is fatal to a little longhaired dog.

Heatstroke symptoms include a dazed look and rapid, shallow panting with a high fever. The dog's gums will be bright red. This is one situation where you must act before going to the veterinarian. Immediately lower the dog's temperature with cool water or with a mixture of cool water and alcohol. Rush it to the *nearest* veterinary hospital, immediately.

Your Pomeranian and Medical Care

Old Age and Your Pomeranian

Aging is a natural process that will affect both you and your Pomeranian. The bouncy puppy will give way to the young adult, who will become the mature dog, who will become your long-time companion and old friend. Pomeranians normally have a long life span, but aging is not without its adjustments. As your Pomeranian begins to reach 8 or 9 years of age (some dogs age more quickly than others) certain changes will become evident. Your Pom may begin to slow down a little, sleep more, and generally be less active.

Your Pom may begin to experience certain age-related health problems with its teeth and gums, bowels and bladder, eyesight and hearing. Your good preventive care that began in puppyhood, along with regular veterinarian visits can forestall or delay many of these concerns, but if your Pom lives long enough, some age-related troubles will present themselves.

Health Areas to Watch

Teeth

Throughout the life of your Pomeranian, tartar buildup on its teeth will be a problem. Feeding a premium quality dry dog food will serve as an abrasive to help keep your Pom's teeth clean. Other chewing toys, nylon bones, and similar products will also help, but as with humans, brushing from puppyhood on will help keep down plaque and tartar. If you pay attention to your Pom's teeth early on and then consistently thereafter, your dog will have healthier teeth and fresher breath.

If you will use one of the new canine oral care kits (a special tooth brush and veterinary dentifrice) on a regular basis, your Pom will have a much better chance to avoid dental problems later on. Weak, loose, or decayed teeth and gum problems can plague older Pomeranians and cause other health problems. You could have your groomer or veter-

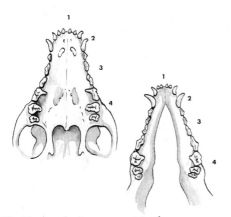

The Pomeranian's permanent teeth.
Upper Teeth: 1. six incisors 2. two canines 3. eight premolars 4. four molars
Lower Teeth: 1. six incisors 2. two canines 3. eight premolars 4. six molars

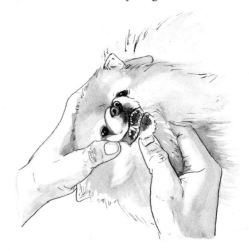

Through regular inspections for tartar and plaque buildup and good dental care, you help your Pomeranian avoid many tooth problems.

inarian begin early in your pup's life to clean its teeth. Check your Pom's teeth on a weekly basis. Don't neglect your Pom's "pearlies." You'll regret it if you do.

Eyes

The Pomeranian's eyes are large and prominent. Eye care, under normal conditions, is not a major problem. Always use good preventive measures such as avoiding any sharp objects at eye level that might harm your Pomeranian. Angry cats have already been mentioned for their danger potential.

You may, on occasion, see some mucouslike matter collecting in the corners of your dog's eyes. This is of no real consequence. Use a tissue and gently wipe the material out of the eyes.

As with other medical matters, use common sense. If your Pom begins to have excessive eye discharge, redness, or evident discomfort, consult your veterinarian. As with humans, Pomeranians can suffer from exposure to chemical fumes (household cleaners, exterminators, etc.) or to smoke (cigarette or fireplace). Just a little awareness of what life

is like at its level of under 12 inches will help you protect your Pom's eyes.

Older dogs, including older Pomeranians, sometimes develop cataracts, a thick opaqueness of or involving the lens. You will notice a gradual "clouding" of the eye. Cataracts can be part of the aging process. Other than the cosmetic aspects and some vision impairment, cataracts are not usually serious.

Ears

Much of the regular observation you do to guard against ear mites will help you monitor overall ear health. Your groomer and your veterinarian will also help you prevent problems here. If the ears begin to show inflammation or the dog repeatedly is bothered by its ears, there may be an infection. Don't delay in seeking professional care.

If your Pom has access to a wooded area, you need to know that the ears are a favorite target area for ticks. Always check for these critters if your Pom has been where ticks may be lurking.

Nails

Part of the consistent care regimen for your Pomeranian will be regular attention to its toe-

The eyes of the Pomeranian are among its most prominent features. You can help protect your dog's eyes by having regularly scheduled eye exams done by your veterinarian, by eliminating any eye hazards in your home, and by keeping the eyes clean.

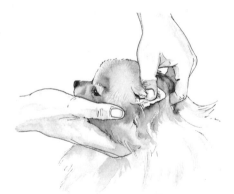

Check for ear mites frequently. Give your Pomeranian's ears a thorough look to spot any problems that may require veterinary attention.

nails. Beginning while your Pom is still a puppy, its nails should be kept trimmed. By starting early and gently, you Pom will not fear nail trimming, which it will need on a monthly basis for the rest of its life. Failure to keep the nails at an appropriate length can result in painful lameness for a Pom whose way of walking depends on its being up on its tiptoes.

Your groomer can handle the nail trimming during the monthly grooming session. But you can trim the nails yourself with a good pair of clippers and keep them neat with a good nail file. Get your groomer or veterinarian to show you how to use them. Practice on round toothpicks to learn to cut off just the tip of the nail; you must avoid the "quick" or center of the nail which will bleed if it is cut. (You can use styptic powder if you do accidentally cut the nail too short.)

How to Administer Medicine

While much of your Pom's health care will rest in the hands of your veterinarian, being

Trimming your Pomeranian's nails is not difficult. Ask your groomer or veterinarian to show you how to do it. Remember, if you cut the nails yourself, trim only the outer points. Avoid cutting into the quick.

able to administer the prescription medicines is good to know. Your Pomeranian may not like taking medicine and may spit out pills and capsules. One way to get pills, like monthly heartworm medication, into the Pom is by hiding them in some treat item. One Pom breeder used a small piece of bread smeared with smooth peanut butter to make the medicine go down.

The direct approach is to simply open your Pom's mouth, tilting the head back just a little way and placing the pill as far back on the tongue as you can. Close the dog's mouth and wait for it to swallow. *It is important not to just casually toss the pill into the dog's mouth or tilt the head back too far; the pill could be caught in the windpipe instead of going down the throat.* Liquid medicine is administered in a similar way by tilting the head back only slightly and pouring the liquid dosage into the back of the dog's mouth. Tilting the head too far back can also cause possible choking as the liquid may flow into the windpipe.

Euthanasia

When in the natural course of your Pom's life, age, infirmity, or terminal illness makes that life a painful, negative experience for your Pomeranian, you have a difficult decision to make. It is never easy to say goodbye to a loving pet whose life has made yours so much brighter, just by being there. It will be even harder to see that same loving pet in constant pain as it goes about even basic daily activities.

Discuss this with your veterinarian, whom I hope has taken care of your dog for a long time and personally cares about it too. Euthanasia, although a painful decision for you, is painless and humane for your old friend. It should be considered when your Pomeranian can no longer experience even the simple joy of being because it is enduring a life of increasing discomfort, disability, and suffering.

Training Your Pomeranian

The Key to Training— Understanding Pack Behavior

Your cute, cuddly Pomeranian puppy is a pack animal just like the wolf, the sled dog, or the foxhound. Pack behavior is a natural, integral part of your puppy and the key to teaching it to be a well-trained good canine citizen.

The pack, in simple terms, is a canine caste system where each member has and knows its place. The pack provides security and a sense of belonging that is crucial to a well-adjusted dog. Positioning in the pack hierarchy is usually based on physical strength and experience. Within it the strongest male with the most savvy fills the role of "alpha" or first male.

The alpha dog leads the pack. He adjudicates differences between pack members, enforces his will on the pack and helps train the young or inexperienced in what is expected of them as pack members. He stays the alpha dog as long as he is the strongest. You will have to perform this role for your Pomeranian and your family will have to serve as the pack members. Your puppy will have already been taught pack behavior by its mother and litter mates. You and the other members of your household will be a logical (and necessary) extension of what the mother dog began.

Training will be much more easily accomplished if you follow the example of your Pom's mother. She taught the puppy, almost from the moment of its birth, lessons it would need to survive. As the pup grew, she reprimanded it, loved it, and instructed it in a pattern that you can and should follow. That is:

1. She admonished the puppy *quickly* for any misdeeds (while the puppy, with its short attention span, could identify action with outcome).

2. She corrected the puppy *fairly,* neither overreacting nor underreacting to its misdeed.

3. She was *consistent* in her treatment of the puppy. A particular behavior did not get a loving lick one time and a warning growl the next.

4. She went about her training *without anger*. She didn't savagely attack the puppy for a misdeed nor did she bark at it endlessly in an effort to "verbalize" the puppy into correct behavior.

5. She showed that she *loved* the puppy and made it feel secure, even if it had done something that had warranted correction earlier in the day. She didn't withhold love to force the puppy to act correctly.

There is much to learn from the lessons taught by the mother. Not only does your puppy already understand these lessons, but the lessons worked for her and will work for you!

When you take your Pom from its mother and the security of the litterpack you should immediately move to fill this gap. You and your family would do well to understand the role of the pack in the emotional well-being of your Pomeranian. You (or your designated person) must become the alpha dog to help this youngster learn its lessons. Your Pomeranian will want to please you after it knows that you love it and will care for it. How your Pom goes about learning what it must do to please you is up to you. The puppy won't learn these lessons by simple osmosis, it must be trained.

The Pomeranian, like its cousin the Keeshond (shown here), is often at its best in the spotlight at dog shows. It has been said that the Pom seems to understand and relish showing off for the judge and the crowd.

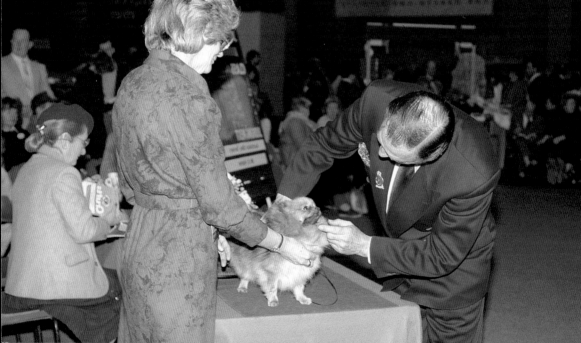

Training Your Pomeranian

When to Begin Training

Some lessons, like housebreaking and basic rules can begin immediately. More involved training should begin between 5 and 8 months based on your dog's own timetable. Some pups are ready earlier than others. Don't push your puppy to be an "early bloomer" (in a form of behavior often identified with backstage mothers or little league fathers). Let the pup learn what it can in the security of the home, and when it seems ready (physically and mentally mature) for further training, move on to the next step. Always remember the mother dog's training example: (a) quickness of reprimand, (b) fairness, (c) consistency, (d) without anger, (e) in an environment where affection and security was clearly in evidence.

Essentials of Training

1. You and your puppy will need a regularly set time (perhaps a couple of times a day) free from distractions (other dogs, running children, etc.). This time should be short (not more than 15 minutes), and while enjoyable it should be work-time not play-time.

2. You need to have a clear idea (perhaps discussed with other members of your family) of what you want your Pomeranian to learn. Consistency is important. You can't be correcting behavior that everyone else in the family ignores or even rewards!

Praising your Pomeranian when it does what you want it to do is the best possible reward you can give your pet. Appropriate and consistent praise also serves as a positive reinforcement that makes the entire training process much easier.

3. You are the boss, the alpha dog. Use a stern tone of voice during the training sessions to differentiate from other times when you and the Pom are together. This is an authoritarian hat, but not a drill sergeant's hat. These sessions should never be conducted when you are angry at the dog, your spouse, or your boss.

4. Each session should be conducted as a class. Learning is the objective. If the command "come" is to be taught today, don't try to get into the variations of "fetch" or "roll over." Stay to the subject. Review previous lessons, praise the dog when it does something right. Correct *each* time it doesn't do what it should, but make sure that the dog understands the desired action. If you can't get a lesson across, go back to something the dog does well. Do that several times, then praise the dog and stop for the day.

5. Use appropriate praise for a successful behavior. This doesn't mean the dog does what you want one time and then you rough

◄ Whether "strutting its stuff" in the show ring or carrying out commands in an obedience trial, the Pomeranian always has a sense of presence that draws the attention of onlookers.

house for the rest of the time. Praise effectively, but save play for later (allow a few minutes of lag time between the lesson and play time so that the two are not confused).

6. Correct misdeeds immediately while you can. Cause the puppy to identify the action or misdeed with your reprimand. Don't attempt to punish the dog for something done some time ago. It won't remember or understand why you are reprimanding (free-floating reprimands don't do anything but confuse the dog when you do want to change its behavior).

7. Be patient and never lose your temper. Ranting and raving or whipping the dog can ruin the puppy's trust in you. Remember the lack of anger the mother dog used with the puppies.

Discipline

As mentioned previously, your Pomeranian should never be the victim of severe physical punishment. If you follow the previous training-session design, a stern voice using the word "no" in a firm manner will convey your displeasure.

Some dogs will test the limits of your control and your ability to be the alpha dog. Just because a Pom is small doesn't mean this testing won't take place. Counter any such behavior immediately and consistently. You are the alpha dog and as such you can't put up with such behavior.

Setting the Stage for Training

Your puppy will need to learn its name early in your relationship. If your dog is a registered Pom from a long line of champions it may have an impressive (or even pretentious) formal name. It is amazing how a tiny puppy who just fits in your hand could have a moniker such as "Mandrake's Lothar of Ham-

bletonian." It will need a short name that will be its "call name," preferably of one syllable. Name your puppy and stick with that name. Have your family stick with it. If the dog's call name is Mike, call him Mike, not Mickey or Mikey Poo. Your dog definitely needs to know what its name is in order for training to begin.

Housebreaking

You have already begun to help your puppy learn in this area. Your puppy will want to please you, but it will also have the basic need to eliminate wastes. Your task is to help the puppy learn how to please you by eliminating its wastes at a certain place and time of your choosing.

No matter how much your Pomeranian puppy may want to please you, it will have only limited bladder control until it reaches between 4 and 6 months of age. Until then, don't expect total housebreaking to take place. That does not mean that you don't provide a

Never use physical punishment or rub the puppy's nose in any messes it might make. A firm "no" will convey your displeasure, won't scare the puppy, and you won't have to clean up the Pom afterwards.

solid foundation for the time when the dog's physical functioning catches up with its desire to please you.

Crate-training takes advantage of the Pomeranians innate desire to keep its den clean (see Crate Training Hints). It is also a very excellent way to help housebreak your puppy. But it does require a regular plan for feeding and for walks. When crate-training is combined with such a plan and loads of praise when the puppy does what you want, it will work well.

Some basic understanding of when your puppy will need to relieve itself is essential. Take the puppy out to the established relief area after it eats or drinks (additional food causes pressure on the colon and bladder). Go out the first thing each morning and after naps during the day. Go out after a long, strenuous play session. Go out as late at night as possible. By all means, take the pup out if it begins to show signs of wanting to defecate or urinate, such as staying near the door, circling and sniffing, and a general uneasy look.

Sometimes you will read the signs and get the puppy outside just in time. When the puppy relieves itself in the appropriate place, praise should be immediate. Stay with the puppy until it does eliminate and you have praised it. Make an extra effort to help the puppy learn the behavior you expect of it. Never scold the dog at the appointed elimination location. Give the puppy positive reinforcement at this all important site. Don't confuse your Pom by sending mixed messages.

Never strike the puppy if it has an accident. A firm "No" will let the puppy know the displeasure that the action merits. *Never* rub the puppy's nose in urine or excrement. This will not only discourage positive behavior, but then you have to clean up the puppy. In letting the Pom know what bad behavior is and in praising good behavior, you highlight the rewarded act and make it the memorable thing.

Regular feeding times with a premium quality food will help you anticipate when the puppy needs to go. Additionally, the premium dog food will produce firmer stools with less volume that will be easier to clean up if a mess does happen. Avoid table scraps and treats. They can only upset the nutritional balance of the quality food. Also feed only at the set times; do not leave food out for your puppy all day. Your Pomeranian puppy will do well on three to four meals a day.

As mentioned, your Pom will not want to soil its den. Its mother gave your pup early lessons in keeping the den area clean. Take advantage of this innate behavior with regular meals and regular walks; you will help the puppy win your praise and avoid the stern "No" that comes from mistakes.

Whereas crate training is probably the most efficient way to housebreak your Pom, it may not work equally well for those who cannot be at home with their puppy during the day. For these people, a slower method works—paper training.

Paper-training is built on confining the puppy to some easily cleaned room (a kitchen, a bathroom, or a laundry room). It does not work particularly well with outside training because the puppy is given two "right" places to go, but it may be necessary for those whose schedules cannot revolve around the puppy. It also is effective for those who live in highrise apartments and others to whom rapid trips outside are impractical or impossible.

Three separate areas within the puppy's confined room are needed; the elimination area, the food and water area and the den area containing the carrier/crate/cage. The area set aside for waste elimination is covered with several layers of newspaper. The puppy is encouraged to use this part of the room, the part with the newspapers. Praise is given every time the puppy does what it is supposed to do in the right area. Pomeranians and other breeds do not like to soil *either* their sleeping areas or their eating areas, neither of which should be too close to the waste area. When the pup uses the papered area, the top layer is removed and the puppy's scent remains on the lower layers. This encourages the Pom to use the paper again when it needs to relieve itself.

If you need to use the paper-training method, housebreaking will probably take a little longer. Even if you do use it, be sure to walk your puppy early each morning and late each night; don't completely eliminate taking the puppy outside. Also try decreasing the size of the area covered by newspaper gradually, until only a small part of the room is used for elimination. Some trainers advocate taking that small section of paper outside with you to let the pup use it there in the later stages of training.

Whatever method you use to housebreak your Pom, remember to be consistent. Crate-training is a good way to use the "den" influ-

Regular walks with your Pomeranian will become enjoyable to both of you. Several walks a day give your dog needed bladder and bowel breaks, and also provide exercise and a change of scenery.

ence to help the dog learn, but paper-training (if necessary) can be successful combined with regular walks and careful feeding. Both methods depend on consistency and appropriate praise or correction when either is deserved.

The use of the cage/carrier/crate by the Pomeranian gives you the added benefit of being able to regulate the puppy's access to things that might do it harm when you are not around to care for it. Such use for a Pomeranian is not only humane but in keeping with the nature of the breed. As the pup matures, its use of the crate as its own place within your home will remain a constant.

If your puppy does make a mistake, be sure to get that area cleaned up quickly and use an odor-removing cleaner. If the puppy comes upon an area where its scent indicates it has relived itself, it may do so again. If your puppy has inordinate difficulty either with defecation or urination, there may be some medical issue that requires a visit to the veterinarian.

Also remember, if you live in a city and your puppy must use a public street or sidewalk as its elimination area, to curb your dog; pick up and properly dispose of any excreta. Responsibility in this area is yours; many urban laws bear this out.

Basic Training

When your Pomeranian is about 5 months old you can be reasonably sure that it is mature enough to learn the basic obedience commands that will make it a more manageable pet. Unfortunately, some owners of toy breeds fail to give their pets the advantages of training. They seem to feel that their little dog can be carried and therefore be made to do what is required. These people and their pets are missing one of the great joys of human-canine interaction—the ability of the human to find a way to communicate with the canine and shape the canine's behavior, having a good time in the process.

Equipment

You will need a chain or nylon training collar of the type commonly called a "choke-chain." This is the most effective and humane way to train your Pom. When you use the collar correctly the collar does not choke the dog, it merely provides restraining, correcting pressure when given a quick tug upward. This gets the pup's attention and also serves as a correcting method. The quick tug and the stern word "No," let the puppy know it has done wrong. The collar will need to be large enough to go over your Pom's head at its widest part with about one inch to spare but not much more. This collar is generally used for training only. Before beginning the lesson, swap your Pom's regular collar (the one attached to its personal identification and rabies vaccination tags) for the training collar.

With the training collar you will need a 1/2- to 1-inch (1.3–2.5 cm) wide leash (or lead) measuring about 6 feet (1.8 m) long. The lead can be leather, web, or nylon. It will need to have a swivel snap at one end for fastening through the ring on the training collar. At the other end, the lead should have a comfortable hand loop. This lead is, of course, longer than your normal walking leash.

You should familiarize your puppy with the training collar and with the lead in a carefully orchestrated way so that the puppy will not come to fear or dislike either the collar or the lead. In a large room where there are no obstacles to snag the lead and frighten the puppy, let your Pom run around with the training collar on and the lead trailing along behind. This will give the puppy the feel of the weight of the collar and lead before training time actually rolls around.

There are five basic commands: "sit," "down," "stay," "heel," and "come." With these five skills firmly in its repertoire, your Pom will be a better pet or could even pursue further training in the obedience ring if it has the aptitude and you are so inclined. Be sure to issue clear, one-word commands to your dog, such as "Sit." Use the dog's name before each command and be authoritarian in your tone. Use the same tone each time. Don't confuse your dog by using two commands at one time, such as "sit-down." Also remember the keys to canine learning are wrapped up in four rules: (1) praise enthusiastically, (2) correct fairly and immediately, (3) practice consistent repetition, and (4) don't lose your temper.

The Five Basic Obedience Commands

Sit

The "sit" is a good command. Your pup already knows how to sit, all you need to do

The "sit" command is accomplished by pressing gently on the dog's hindquarters with your left hand while you gently pull up on the lead to lift the dog's head. Always repeat the word "sit" to help your Pomeranian associate the action with the command.

69

is teach it when and where to do so. With the training collar on and attached to the lead, place your Pom on your left side next to your left leg, while holding the lead in your right hand. In one continuous, gentle motion pull the pup's head up with the lead as you push its hindquarters down with your left hand, giving a firm command "Sit" as you do so.

When the Pom is in the sitting position, lavishly praise it. Using the concept of consistent repetition, repeat the lesson until your Pom sits down without its rear end being pushed. Remember to keep the same upward pressure on the lead to prevent a sit from becoming a belly flop. If the dog shifts in position, use your left hand to move it back to where it belongs. Keep doing this exercise until the Pomeranian associates the word "sit" and your tone with the praise it gets if it sits down. Soon the Pom will sit upon hearing the word alone without the rear-end push or the raised lead. Always use praise liberally. Make the praise and the lesson stick out in your Pom's mind.

Keep your training time brief. Initially don't leave the young dog in the sitting position long enough to bore it. Gradually increase the time for sitting. Remember consistent repetition with praise and correction will help your pup learn. You may have to begin again each time for a while. Your Pom will learn more quickly with several brief consistent sessions than with one, long, drawn-out session.

Stay

Do not attempt to teach "stay" until your pup is doing well with "sit." The stay is begun from the sit and without that foundation, the command cannot be mastered.

To begin your part of the stay command, you must place your dog in a regular sitting position on your left. You keep some pressure on the lead in your right hand to keep the Pom's head up. Giving the clear, authoritative

The "stay" command begins with the Pomeranian in the "sit" position. The "stay" can only be learned after the dog has mastered the "sit." Give the command "stay," stepping away from the dog, right foot first, as you bring the palm of your left hand down and in front of the dog's face.

command "Stay" you step away from the dog (moving your right foot first). At the same time, you bring the palm of your left, hand down and in front of the Pomeranian's face. Your command, the stepping away (moving the right foot first), and the hand signal must be simultaneous and done exactly the same way in each repetition.

Keep eye contact with your dog and repeat the stay command (in the same firm tone as before). Don't really expect long stays initially. Praise the puppy for its stays whatever their length, but if it moves toward you take it back to the starting point, make it sit and start again with consistent repetition. Patience is the rule here. Your dog loves you and wants to come and be with you. If your pup has trouble with the stay, don't wear it down trying, go back to the sit, a command which it can do well and enthusiastically praise the puppy.

Training Your Pomeranian

Each time the pup obeys the stay command praise it. You will be able to gradually move further away and the puppy will eventually get the idea. Introduce the release word "Okay" in a cheerful happy way when you want to let the puppy know that it can now come to you and be praised.

Because of the conflicts the puppy feels—wanting to please you and wanting to be with you—the stay is fairly difficult but with patience and consistency you will see your Pomeranian master it.

Heel

Now that the training collar and lead are part of your dog's experience, you can teach it to "heel," a most useful command. Begin heel training with your Pomeranian on your left side, its head next to your left foot, in the sit position. Holding the lead in your right hand and leading with your left foot, step forward saying in your firm, authoritative "alpha" voice, "Heel!" Use the dog's name

The "heel" command is a very useful part of your Pomeranian's education. As with the "stay," the "heel" begins with the dog in a sitting position. Heeling training begins with the dog on your left side with the lead held in your right hand.

to begin the command as in, "Mike, heel." If your Pom doesn't move out when you do, snap the lead sharply against your leg and repeat the command walking away as you do. As soon as your Pom catches up with you, praise it but keep moving, using encouraging praise as long as it stays with you in proper position.

When you stop, tell your dog to sit. As the Pomeranian becomes more experienced in heeling it will learn to sit on its own when you stop. Don't let your Pom lag behind or run ahead or edge around to face you. The purpose of the heel command is not just to walk your dog but to position the dog on your left and teach it to move and stop when you move and stop. The ultimate goal of heeling would be to have the dog accomplish this without the lead.

Don't drag your Pom with you just to cover some distance. Go back to the sit and start again. This heel command is tough for some dogs to learn. Continue your use of tugs on the lead to keep your Pom moving and keep its head in line with your left leg. Pomeranians are intelligent and most can pick up heeling in a few consistent, patient lessons.

Down

"Down" begins with the "sit" and the "stay." Using the lead in an opposite movement from the upward pressure used with the sit and the stay, pull down on the lead with your right hand, presenting the palm of your left hand with a downward motion while clearly giving the command "Down." The small size of the Pom makes this easy to do. If the dog doesn't want to lie down, put the lead under your left foot and pull up on it gently forcing the Pom's head downward. Again use the hand signal and the command, "Down." Once the pup is in the down position heap on the praise. You can help your pup just a bit in the early lessons for this command by using your left hand, as in the sit command,

71

but push on the back rather than on the hind-quarters. It is the downward direction that this command strives to emphasize, but it should be used in conjunction with the stay. The ultimate goal is to cause the Pom to go straight down on its stomach and remain there until released by the okay command from you.

The down can be a very useful and important command used to stop your Pom in its tracks when it might be heading for trouble or danger. Practice the down together with sit and stay; always make sure that your Pomeranian is rewarded when it stays put in the down position. Using the credo of consistent repetition you should be able to gradually increase the length of the down and even leave the Pom's line of sight and expect it to remain in place. As with the stay, your Pom should not move about. Correct it if it does, praise it if it doesn't.

Come

The "come" command may seem simple, but there are several important elements to it. Enthusiasm and use of the dog's name and the command with wide open arms will let your puppy know you really want to be with it. This seems like a natural behavior; yet, so many people foolishly call their dogs and then scold, punish, or even whip them. To an intelligent Pomeranian puppy the command "Come" issued by you (or any of your family), then followed by a reprimand could cause this natural behavior to be unlearned quickly. *Never* call your dog to you and correct or punish it. If the dog must be corrected, you go to the dog and do it.

Always heap loads of praise on your Pomeranian when it comes at your call. Remember that the dog must learn that come, like the other commands, must be obeyed immediately each and every time. If your dog is a little stubborn or inattentive to the command, give the lead (which of course is still in use) a firm but gentle tug to get movement in your direction started. This method will work, especially when combined with the authoritative command from you as the alpha leader and the warm tones and friendly gesturing that follow it. If not, a little sharper tug used with the command can be used. You have your puppy on a 6-foot (2 m) lead but a longer lead can be used—up to 20 feet (6 m)—to reinforce the command from a greater distance.

One point in the come command differs from the others. This command does not need to be repeated over and over again during a lesson. Use it when you are working on the other lessons or when your dog is involved in play or something else. Always expect the dog to obey this command quickly and praise the dog when it complies.

Remember that saying "Come" and then reprimanding is an excellent way to untrain your dog. Teach that to your family. While discussing this with your family, let each person learn all the different commands and the correct "hows" and "whys" of each part. This will make things much saner for your puppy who can't possibly learn when it is getting conflicting usages of the same word from different members of its "pack."

Obedience Classes

If, for whatever reason, you can't seem to teach your Pomeranian (which is unusual) don't hesitate to enlist the help of a professionally run obedience school or class. Another option is a local dog club where obedience lessons are frequently offered. Recognize that much of what will be taught in these classes will be aimed at helping you train yourself to train your dog. There are many other things that a smart Pom can learn beyond the basic commands discussed here. You may want to give your pup (or adult dog) a chance at higher education.

Training Your Pomeranian

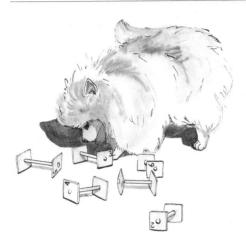

Obedience classes, either those run by professional dog trainers or those under the guidance of a local kennel or obedience club, will help you help your bright Pomeranian further its education.

Obedience trials have become one of the fastest growing dog-related activities in the United States. You and your Pomeranian may find much enjoyment in the hard work and challenges of the obedience ring.

Obedience Trials

Obedience trials have become one of the fastest growing dog-related activities in the United States. If you and your Pomeranian are suited for this activity you may want to see what obedience trials are all about.

You can get a copy of the rules from the AKC. This will give you all you need to know about Novice Class competitions. Obedience work isn't for every dog owner or for every dog, but for those who want to learn the various titles (CD, Companion Dog; CDX, Companion Dog Excellent; UD, Utility Dog; OT Ch, Obedience Trial Champion) it can be a wonderful undertaking.

The United Kennel Club (UKC) and the Canadian Kennel Club (CKC) also sanction obedience trials. Pomeranians are eligible for these trials also.

Crate Training Hints

- Maintain a realistic and positive attitude about the use of crates/cages/carriers and the positive role they can play in providing a "den" for your Pomeranian.
- Obtain a large enough crate/cage/carrier to comfortably serve as a den for your Pom when it is an adult. Make a movable, temporary partition to keep the den just the right size as your puppy grows.
- Locate such a den in an out-of-the-way, but not isolated, place in a part of the household always in use but away from any temperature fluctuations that would make it uncomfortable at times.
- Put the puppy in the crate/cage/carrier for naps and when it must be left unattended for several hours. Upon your return, immediately take the puppy outside to the elimination location. Praise the puppy when

it defecates or urinates and go right back inside with the pup.

- Use the stern alpha-leader, authoritative voice to quiet any whining or barking of the pup as it is being placed in the makeshift den.
- Do not praise the puppy for about ten minutes after it is let out of the cage/crate/carrier. To do so will make getting out more of a reward than you want it to be.
- During training put the puppy back in its den after about 30 minutes outside of it and make the puppy quiet down. Remember to delay praise for a few minutes when you let the puppy out. Through consistent reinforcement the amount of time you can leave the Pom in can be extended.
- Always keep a mat or towel in its den along with a favorite chewing toy to make it a comfortable place.
- In order to cut down on possible spillage do not put food or water in the cage/crate/carrier.
- Make sure your family and frequent visitors to your house fully understand the importance of crate training and how it must be done.

Barking Behavior

As mentioned earlier, Pomeranians are alert, vocal little dogs who show an interest in everything and everyone. When this interest takes the form of unwarranted barking, some training techniques need to be applied to the problem. Again, the prevention is much better than the cure.

Beginning with the very young puppy on his first night with you, if you let the sad crying of a baby Pom cause you to pick it up repeatedly then you are training that puppy to do something that later you will not like.

Just as you should never encourage begging behavior by feeding tidbits at the dinner table, you can keep yourself from teaching unwarranted barking in much the same way. Simply don't respond to barking when you don't want barking to occur. If your Pom is barking to simply get your attention, steel yourself (and teach this to your family) and ignore the dog. Pay attention to it only when there has been no unwarranted barking. It takes time, but if you are patient and consistent, it works.

Afterword

In this book I try to convey an unvarnished look at a great little breed—the Pomeranian. Also, I bluntly point out that there are a number of responsibilities that go along with Pomeranian ownership. I make no apology for this bluntness—the Pomeranian deserves the best possible treatment.

It is true that much is demanded of a Pom owner. I have made every effort to spell out these demands and get them across. But Pom ownership is not a one-way street. For all your contributions in money, time, attention, and efforts the Pomeranian amply repays in one simple commodity—love.

The love of any dog is a wonderful thing, freely given and without reservation. The love of a Pomeranian is perhaps of an even stronger sort, possibly because more is required in Pom ownership. It is almost as if a Pomeranian knows that its existence is totally dependent on its human being and gives love in equal proportion.

One breeder I spoke with had an interesting sentiment. She said, "One day I would not be at all surprised to see a government regulation requiring a warning label on each and every Pomeranian; 'Caution, loving this little dog may be addictive.' "

History gives a particularly poignant affirmation to this breeder's somewhat facetious remark. Queen Victoria loved all animals, especially dogs. In her long and regal life she gave her royal patronage to over a dozen breeds of dogs, including the Pomeranian. It is safe to say that her acceptance of and enthusiastic support of the little spitz dogs molded and made the Pomeranian. History relates that as England's longest-reigning monarch lay dying she had one final royal command—that Turi, her favorite Pomeranian, be brought to her.

Useful Addresses and Literature

International Kennel Clubs

American Pomeranian Club*
Ms. Audrey Roberts
Corresponding Secretary
1401 S. 10th Street
Leesville, LA 71446

American Kennel Club
51 Madison Avenue
New York, NY 10038

Australian National Kennel Club
Royal Show Ground
Ascot Vale
Victoria Australia

Canadian Kennel Club
2150 Bloor Street West
Toronto, Ontario M6540
Canada

Irish Kennel Club
41 Harcourt Street
Dublin 2
Ireland

The Kennel Club
1-4 Clargis Street
Picadilly
London W7Y 8AB
England

New Zealand Kennel Club
P.O. Box 523
Wellington, 1
New Zealand

*This address may change as a new officer is elected. The latest listing can always be obtained from the American Kennel Club.

Books

In addition to the most recent edition of the official publication of the AKC, *The Complete Dog Book* published by Howell Book House, Inc. in New York, there are:

Alderton, David *The Dog Care Manual*. Barron's Educational Series, Hauppauge, New York, 1986.

Baer, Ted *Communicating with Your Dog*. Barron's Educational Series, Hauppauge, New York, 1989.

Frye, Fredric *First Aid for Your Dog*. Barron's Educational Series, Hauppauge, New York, 1987.

Klever, Ulrich *The Complete Book of Dog Care*. Barron's Educational Series, Hauppauge, New York, 1989.

Pinney, Chris C. *Guide to Home Pet Grooming*. Barron's Educational Series, Hauppauge, New York, 1990.

Ullmann, Hans-J. *The New Dog Handbook*. Barron's Educational Series, Hauppauge, New York, 1985.

Whitney, Leon F. *How to Breed Dogs*. Howell House, Inc., New York, New York, 1973.

Periodicals

The Pom Reader
8848 Beverly Hills Road
Lakeland, Florida 33809

Accredited Boarding Kennels

American Boarding Kennel Association (ABKA) 4574 Galley Road
Suite 400A
Colorado Springs, Colorado 80915

Index

Page numbers in **boldface** indicate color photos.

Index

Index

nature of, 7–8
origin and history, 6–7
sensory organs, 15–16
vocal expression, 12
Potassium, 34
Praise, **28**, 66
Pregnancy, 44
Premium dog food, 35, 37
Preventive care, 51–52
Professional groomer, 38–39
Protein, 33
Puppies, **9**, 18–19
bringing home, 26, 29–30
care of, 47–48
for Christmas, 24
feeding, 36
grooming and, 39
handfeeding, 48
picking up, 23–24
preparing home for, 25–26
selecting, 21–23
socialization of, 48–49
training, 62, 65–75
vaccination schedule, 52
weaning, 48
whelping, 47
Puppy mills, 22
"Puppy-proofing" home, 25–26
Pyometritis, 44

Rabies, 52–53
Red mange, 56
Registration certificate, 23
Roundworms, 54

Scabies, 56
Semimoist food, 35
Sense of smell, 15
Sense of taste, 15–16
Sense of touch, 16
Sensory organs:
eyes and ears, 15
sense of smell and taste, 15–16
sense of touch, 16

Show quality dogs, 20–21
birthing problems, 47
grooming, 38
selecting, 21
Sire, 42–44
"Sit" command, **28**, 69–70
Size, 17, **28**
Skin problems, 56–57
Socialization, 48–49
Sodium, 34
Spaying, 19
Spitz, 6–7
Standard of breed, 16–17
"Stay" command, 70–71
Stools, 35
Stud, 42–43
Stud fee, 43

Tail, 17
Tapeworms, 55
Tartar, 59
Teeth, 17, 59–60
Temperature requirement, puppies, 48
Ticks, 56, 60
Tied mating, 44
Toll-free telephone number (dog foods), 35
Toys, 25
Tracheobronchitis, 53
Training:
barking behavior, 74–75
basic, 68–69
crate training hints, 73–74
discipline, 66
equipment for, 69
essentials of, 65–66
five basic commands, 69–72
housebreaking, 66–68
obedience classes, 72
obedience trials, 73
on arrival home, 29
pack behavior and, 62
setting the stage for, 66
when to begin, 65
Training collar, 69

Travel, 30–31
Treats, 35–36
Trimming, 17, **27**, 60–61

Umbilical cord, 47

Vaccinations:
diseases controlled by, 52–54
schedule for puppies, 52
Vaginal discharge, 41–42
Veterinarian, 51
Victoria (Queen of Great Britain), 6
Virgin, 42
Vitamins, 33
Vocal expression, 12
Vomiting, 57
Vulva, 41

Water, 34
Water bowl, 25
Weaning, 48
Whelping, 44, 47
Whelping box, 44
Worms, 54–55
Written guarantee, 22

79

Perfect for Pet Owners!